DRUM LESS

WITH

GEORGE LAWRENCE STONE

A PERSONAL ACCOUNT ON HOW TO USE *STICK CONTROL*

BY BARRY JAMES WITH JOE MORELLO

Alfred Alfred Music
P.O. Box 10003
Van Nuys, CA 91410-0003
alfred.com

ISBN-10: 1-4706-4339-1
ISBN-13: 978-1-4706-4339-3

Cover photos courtesy of Barbara Haines
1910 George Burt Stone Snare Drum (p. 91) courtesy of Scott Wachsman
All other photos on page 91 courtesy of Barry James
Additional art resources courtesy of Getty Images

CONTENTS

INTRODUCTION BY VIC FIRTH

I enthusiastically endorse this wonderful book, *Drum Lessons with George Lawrence Stone,* written by the great drum instructor Barry James and my good friend Joe Morello.

I had the privilege of taking lessons from George L. Stone, and he was truly a great inspiration. In all my years of teaching, the bible and the backbone of my teaching material were based on Mr. Stone's classic book, *Stick Control.* This new book is a truly accurate training guide and complete reference source for all serious-minded drummers who understand the importance of acquiring strong stick technique. Here is *Stick Control 2.*

While reading through these pages and playing the exercises, I had the feeling I was actually sitting in George Stone's studio, taking another lesson with the "master." It's no wonder that PAS inducted George Stone into its Hall of Fame, and that *Modern Drummer* magazine named *Stick Control* number one in their list of "The 25 Best Drum Books."

Finally, here is a book that is not written by someone who studied with someone who studied with Mr. Stone. Barry James and Joe Morello actually studied with George Stone—you are studying the techniques developed by Mr. Stone first-hand.

While *Stick Control* is arguably the best drum technique book of our time, this companion is sure to become the most important drum technique book for present and future drummers. Study it! Use it! You'll play better! And, you can believe, "This is set in *stone.*"

Vic Firth is a revered name in the drumming community. The company he founded is the leading manufacturer of percussion accessories in the world. Before he founded the company in 1963, Vic taught percussion in the Boston area. He received a bachelor's degree and an honorary doctorate in music from the New England Conservatory of Music. His company supports and endorses many of the best professional drummers of our time.

BACKGROUND

Born in 1886, George Lawrence Stone was the son of drum teacher and drum manufacturer George Burt Stone. In addition to studying drums and xylophone from his father, he also worked in the shop where his dad made some of the best snare drums of that period. George Lawrence said, "If I have had my share of success in teaching others, its origin was in the way my father taught me, and in his counsel, so often repeated: 'If you accept a pupil you accept a responsibility.' In one way or another you've got to go through with them. There's no alibi if you don't.'"

George Lawrence also studied with Harry A. Bower and Frank E. Dodge, and studied music theory at the New England Conservatory of Music, where he eventually taught. Stone joined the musicians union at age 16, becoming its youngest member. By 1910 he was a xylophonist on the Keith Vaudeville Circuit and played timpani and bells with the Boston Festival Orchestra. He also played in the pit of Boston's Colonial Theatre under the baton of Victor Herbert, and was a member of both the Boston Opera Company and the Boston Symphony Orchestra.

After the death of George B. Stone in 1917, George Lawrence took over his father's drum factory, and became the director of the Stone Drum and Xylophone School in Boston. He also wrote articles on drumming technique for *International Musician* and *Jacobs' Orchestra Monthly.* In 1933 he became a founding member of the National Association of Rudimental Drummers (NARD), and served as its president for fifteen years. With the publication of *Stick Control,* George Lawrence became a much sought-after teacher for drummers such as Gene Krupa, Buddy Rich, Sid Catlett, George Wettling, and Lionel Hampton.

Active as a teacher through the 1940s, '50s, and early '60s, Stone taught percussion at Boston University. He is considered one of the first drum technique builders of the 20th century, and he felt it was very important to make music. His theory was that you can be a sculptor by virtue of owning a hammer and chisel, but you don't really sculpt anything until you have the technique to do it. Likewise, before you can do anything "shapely" in music, you've got to have the hands to do it with.

Over the next five decades, other notable Stone students, such as Joe Morello, Vic Firth, and myself, spread the word about Stones' incredible drumming method—teaching it to thousands of drumming enthusiasts.

George Lawrence Stone died on November 19, 1967, at the age of 81. In his eulogy, published in *The Ludwig Drummer,* William F. Ludwig, Sr. said, "George was always helpful to everyone; his motto was 'Service before self.' May he rest in the satisfaction that he did his best for the percussion field for many, many years."

4

JOE MORELLO ON GEORGE LAWRENCE STONE

I started studying with Mr. Stone in the 1940s, when I was still a teenager. I always looked forward to my trips into Boston. Mr. Stone had a dry, New England sense of humor. The time he spent with each student was all business until they got it right; then he would give a student just enough praise to get them motivated to go home and practice. Mr. Stone inspired me at every lesson and showed me the techniques to creative musical expression. *Stick Control* helped me strengthen my hands, and Mr. Stone also showed me how to apply his technique to the drumset! My books, *Master Studies* and *Master Studies, 2*, are my dedicated follow-up to what the master taught me. He called me his "star student," and for that I am forever grateful.

Larry Stone's basic studies were all about a natural approach to drumming. He insisted that there shouldn't be any tension in your body while playing drums. From handholds to the normal rebounding of the sticks, every aspect of playing drums should be relaxed and stress-free.

Stone was also a master of the rudiments. Besides his technique books, *Stick Control* and *Accents and Rebounds*, he also wrote a book called *Military Drum Beats for School and Drum Corps,* and rearranged the famous *Dodge Drum Chart*. He would have me play all 26 rudiments as a warm-up before each lesson. At that time there were only 26 rudiments, but he referred to his book, *Stick Control*, as "A Book of Rudiments." That, it is. You can play the exercises in the book open to closed to open, like a standard rudiment, if you want a challenge. Of course, these exercises, while intended for hand development, can also be played with your feet to build pedal control. On the drumset, you might also try playing all the "rights" on one surface while playing the "lefts" on another. Or, "rights" on the bass drum and "lefts" on the snare. Use your imagination.

Finally, I want to express my gratitude to Barry James. He should be given all the credit for writing this book and bringing the teachings of George Lawrence Stone to a new generation of drummers. I hope I was able to help Barry and share my recollection of the lessons I had with the master drum teacher of our lifetime. Still this book, as originally intended, belongs to George Lawrence Stone. These lessons and lectures are his. In the following pages you will get to know and study with the "master," George (Larry) Stone.

Joe Morello was a jazz drummer best known for his work with the Dave Brubeck Quartet. He was particularly noted for playing in the unusual time signatures employed by that group in such pieces as "Take Five" and "Blue Rondo à la Turk." Popular for their work on college campuses during the 1950s, Brubeck's group reached new heights with Morello. During his career, Joe appeared on over 120 albums, authored several drum books, including *Master Studies*, and also made instructional videos. Joe was the recipient of many awards, including *Playboy* magazine's best drummer award for seven years in a row, and *DownBeat* magazine's best drummer award five years in a row. He was elected to the *Modern Drummer* magazine Hall of Fame in 1988, the Percussive Arts Society Hall of Fame in 1993, and was the recipient of Hudson Music's first TIP (Teacher Integration Program) Lifetime Achievement award.

BARRY JAMES...ABOUT THIS BOOK

The idea for this book started when I attended a clinic by Joe Morello, sponsored by Danny and Beth Gottlieb. After the clinic, Joe and I spoke of our affection for our drum teacher, George Lawrence Stone (or, as Joe called him, Larry Stone). Mr. Stone, we agreed, had trained us well for the careers we both enjoyed.

The discussion turned, of course, to Stone's classic book, *Stick Control.* Joe and I have had the same experience over the years of having to answer questions from students and drum teachers alike—"How do I play such and such page in *Stick Control?*"

Stone once told me "he never intended to publish his many exercises in a book." They were originally written as "handouts" for his private students. With encouragement from Bill Ludwig and others, we now enjoy what is referred to as "The Bible of Drumming."

Still, we are dealing with a book without any explanation on how to play these exercises. Joe jokingly said, "We should write a book on how to play the book." And, that was the beginning of an adventure that took many years and grew into a friendship with the great Joe Morello—one that I will treasure forever.

First, we agreed the teaching should be in Stone's own words, and so I started researching everything I could find that George Stone had written. Fortunately, there was an abundance of articles in the archives of several publications, and so I was able to collect many of them. We culled through Stones' teachings and had regular phone conversations regarding the best way to present these "Lessons with George Lawrence Stone." I also found that Joe Morello must have had a photographic memory. He would remember the details of his drum lessons with Stone, even 60 years later.

When Joe passed away in March of 2011, I put the half-completed manuscript on a shelf for a few years. But, with the urging of friends and family, I decided to finish this book as a tribute to both my beloved drum teacher, George Lawrence Stone, and my friend Joe Morello.

Here, then, are the teachings of George Lawrence Stone.

Barry James' musical career spans over 60 years as a percussionist with jazz groups, show bands, and symphony orchestras. He is recognized as a nationally respected teacher. Many of his students now perform professionally around the world. Barry has taught percussion instruments using The Stone Method throughout his teaching career.

ACKNOWLEDGEMENTS

The author would like to thank all who gave of their time, knowledge, and encouragement to make this book possible.

First, I want to thank Joe Morello. His friendship, dedication, and incredible knowledge of all things Larry Stone were invaluable. To my friends Adrian Zvarych and Dean Slocum, great musicians and scholars who helped me with the initial production of this book. To Stone Percussion Books LLC, Barbara Haines, and the Stone family, thanks for keeping your grandfather's life and work alive. Danny Gottlieb stood behind and encouraged this work for many years. My appreciation to Dave Black for his insightful final editing of this book; and to Alfred for bringing the teachings of Mr. Stone to new and future generations of drummers. Thanks to Tom Cook, webmaster. To the American Federation of Musicians for allowing me access to the articles by George Lawrence Stone published in their *International Musician* magazine.

And, a special thanks to my many students and family for their help, encouragement, and gentle prodding that helped get this book finished. I owe you all. A special thanks to my wife and best friend, Elaine, my sister and brother-in-law, Gayle and Bob, Mom, Betty, Chris and Susan, Tim, Barry, and Dan. And, to my grandchildren, Brian, Kayla, Richard, Michael, Joshua, and little Chris.

WORDS OF WISDOM FROM GEORGE LAWRENCE STONE

There was a poster on Mr. Stone's studio wall, inconspicuous, yet plain enough for all who entered to read. It delineated the three progressive steps for either the student or professional to follow in attaining maximum stick control. The message is reprinted below.

Progressive Steps Towards Stick Control

1. *Precision,* gained through slow motion study and practice.

2. *Endurance,* through endless repetition of figures at normal tempos.

3. *Speed,* and even this practiced below capacity and not until fully warmed up.

"Rhythm is the foundation of all music. The drum, above all others, is the rhythm-producing instrument. Without comprehension and control of rhythmic structure, the drummer cannot maintain tempo and interpret precisely intricate rhythmic patterns. And, if anyone finds it impossible to do two things at once, they should never try to become a drummer. For this individual is constantly over their head, in one way or another, every time they play."—*George Lawrence Stone*

The George L. Stone drum method has become world-renowned for over 80 years since the publication of his classic book, *Stick Control*. It is said that Stone's techniques are considered the gold standard for those who want to master their drumming skills. Indeed, many of the best percussionists in the world have credited Stone's method for their success.

THE BASIC PRINCIPLES OF THE STONE METHOD

Always play in a relaxed, comfortable, and loose fashion. Control of a drumstick begins with a muscularly relaxed action. The sticks should move as if they were a natural extension of your hands. The shoulders, upper arms, forearms, wrists, and fingers should be free to move as needed to produce various dynamics and tempo. Your limbs should feel like well-oiled hinges moving gracefully and smoothly without allowing any tension whatsoever to enter your body.

The Power Stroke Versus the Rebound Stroke

While there is certainly a place for the "power stroke," particularly for *fff* (loud) musical phrasing, Stone preferred the rebound stroke. Like bouncing a rubber ball, the drumstick, when dropped onto a surface, will rebound back up to you. There is a force of nature at work here. For every action there is a reaction. Using this concept, you only need to control the hit and to rebound with the proper handhold. The very nature of a looser hold will help relieve tension. Stone also suggested practicing in a continuous motion while "bouncing" the sticks. This can be accomplished first by using the wrists as well as the fingers. Next, work out your rebounding skills using your arms, as well as your shoulders. Stone believed that a drummer should not keep their arms still and rely only on the wrists and fingers. He taught a composite movement for the basic strokes in which all the parts (shoulders, arms, wrists, and fingers) moved together.

Placement of the Snare Drum

Stone suggested that the snare drum, whether you're in a standing position or performing on a drumset, should be placed approximately 1 to 2 inches below "belly-button" height. In addition, the snare drum should be flat (if playing matched grip), or tilted so the higher side of the drum is on the left side (for a right-handed drummer) using traditional grip. This will allow the sticks to strike at the same angle, regardless of your favored grip. Next, Stone taught the importance of playing at the same volume with both hands; be sure the distance between your strokes is precise and even, and control your strokes to get a consistent volume and rhythm between the hands.

Many Ways to Study *Stick Control*

Stone referred to his *Stick Control* book as "a book of 1,000 rudiments." And, because of his approach teaching from his book, many thousands of exercises can actually be produced.

First and foremost, practice each exercise 20 times. This will build your endurance and muscle memory. If you make a mistake, go back and start over.

Next, Stone had his students play each page of exercises three times. For instance, we would be assigned to practice page 5 (first for accuracy). Then, at the next lesson, we would go on to page 6 (for accuracy) but would again practice page 5 (this time for speed). The tempo used to replay page 5 would depend on our comfort level. We would always use a metronome to not only check our accuracy, but to help push up the tempos as we progressed. Then, on the third week, we would go on to page 7 for accuracy (while practicing page 6 for speed), and then practice page 5 once again, but this time with our feet (see below, "Speed on the Pedals"). So, as you can see, each page was practiced for three consecutive lessons. First, for accuracy, next for speed, and then again to train our feet. This process was consistent throughout the entire *Stick Control* book.

Additionally, students were encouraged to play each exercise in the mode of a standard rudiment (for example, open to closed to open). We would start slowly, then gradually and evenly get faster until we reached our fastest ability. We would hold that tempo for at least 10 seconds and then gradually and evenly slow back down to the beginning tempo. This is a great endurance builder.

For extra practice, Stone would have his students combine the exercises in *Stick Control* by turning two-measure exercises into four-measure exercises, and then those four-measure exercises into eight-measure exercises, etc. For example, we would take page 5 and combine exercise 1 with exercise 13. Or, exercise 1 with exercise 24, etc. You get the idea! By combining the many exercises in the book, thousands of possibilities can be produced. Stone would also have his advanced students purchase a second copy of *Stick Control* so they could open any page in the first book and, beside it, open any page in the second book. By using this method, we could combine any exercise on any page in one book with any exercise on any page in the second book.

Speed on the Pedals

Many of today's drummers are arming their drumsets with two bass drums. This allows them to play rolls and other rudimental flourishes with the bombastic effects only double bass drums can produce. The question then becomes, "How can you train your feet to perform as well as your hands?"

The number one method is through concentrated practice on the action of the foot itself, by operating your pedal at various tempos for an extended period each day. In case a daily diet of several thousand thuds from your bass drum disturbs your neighbors, tap your foot similarly on the floor.

It is important to set up your bass drums so that both feet reach the pedals comfortably, without stretching them out or crowding them in too close. It is generally understood that the spring on your pedals should be loose rather than tight.

The muscles employed in pedaling are neither accustomed to, nor prepared for, the terrific bursts of speed called for in modern up tempos. Consequently, special practice routines are called for.

Cramps in the involved muscles are quite common in the beginning, but an occasional gentle massage when the going gets tough will aid in "rubbing the cramps out."

Some of the current two-bass drum experts have found they can attain great two-foot speed by playing exercises primarily intended for the hands (drumsticks) with their feet. Try "footing" instead of "sticking." And, practice both with your heels down on the pedal board and then heels up with the balls of your feet.

Try the exercises in *Stick Control* and see what I mean. Obviously, not all the exercises in the book can be played with your feet, specifically those pertaining to closed (buzz) rolls. Most of the other *Stick Control* exercises, however, are doable with your feet.

Now you can see how *Stick Control* holds an infinite number of possibilities. For this reason, I strongly suggest that students master these techniques.

NOTE: The lessons and lectures presented in this book are "composites" of George Stone's actual lessons. Stone would spend an hour lesson detailing a particular aspect of a given subject. He would then continue his teaching of this subject at the next lesson (or even a month later). Here, we are combining his teachings on a given subject into one or more sections of our composite lessons. Therefore, it's best that you go through this book slowly and methodically. These combined lessons are not intended to be studied in one sitting. Take on each aspect of each lesson, and don't bite off more than you can chew.

NOTE: Stone hand wrote all the drum exercises for his published articles and student handouts. Unfortunately, due to their age and condition, we were not able to use all of these handwritten exercises. We did, however, reproduce them exactly as originally written using music software. And, we have included some of Stone's handwritten exercises in the back of the book for you to see.

NOTE: Over the years drummers have speculated if there are more single-beat combinations than just the 72 exercises on pages 5, 6, and 7 of *Stick Control*. Yes, in fact, there are. On the next page, (thanks to Joe Morello) you'll find a fourth page of single-beat combinations that Stone intended to be a handout for his private students.

Single-Beat Combinations...The Missing Page

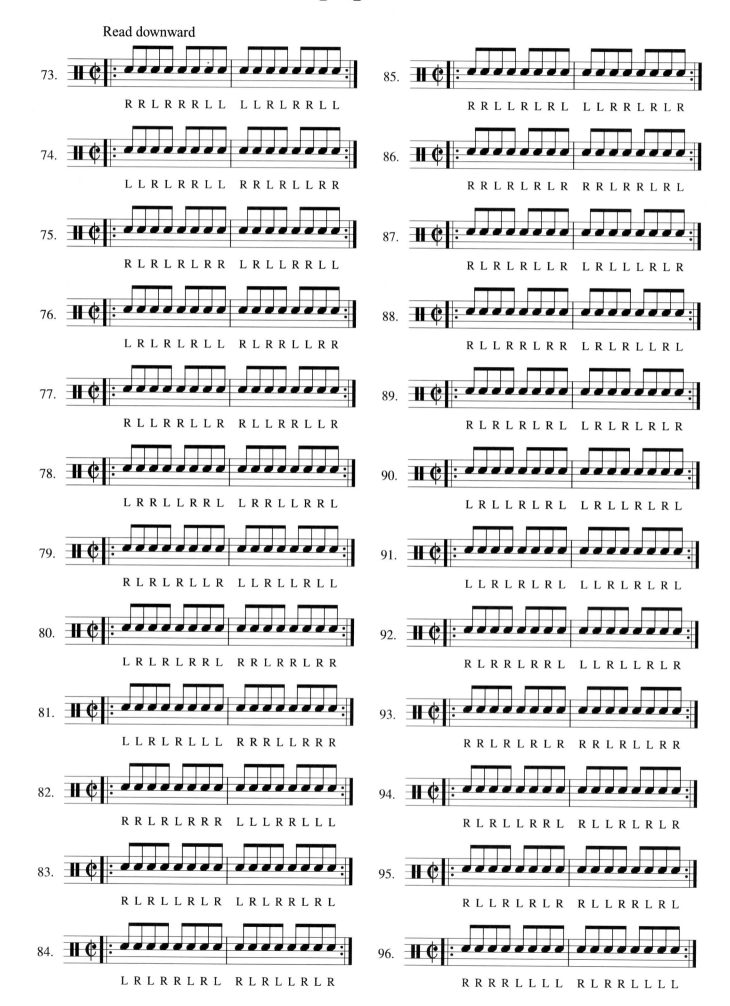

Practice Pad Versus Snare Drum

Drummers often ask about the relative merits of using a practice pad versus the drum itself.

Stone believed the bulk of daily practice should be done on the pad, as it is more difficult to play on a pad than on a drum. Hence, pad practice develops the playing muscles more fully and in less time. Since the drum tone covers many inequalities, indistinguishable except to the most alert ear, mistakes made on the pad are more apparent, and therefore more readily corrected.

However, as we all know, there is a decided difference between touch on a pad and touch on the drumhead. So, for drum touch and sensitivity, final practice must be done on the drum.

The Stone Level System is intended to help you place your sticks in the correct position so 1) you can play them again immediately as called for in the musical pattern and 2) you can execute accents and other dynamics.

The Level System consists of three different heights for lifting the sticks above the surface of the drum and/or practice pad as follows: a full stroke (18 inches above the playing surface), a half stroke (9 inches above the playing surface), and a tap stroke (3 inches above the playing surface), though Stone often reminded his students that these levels are flexible. For example, the full stroke could be 15 inches, while the half stroke could be 7 inches, and the tap stroke 2 inches. It's all relative and a personal preference. Just be consistent.

Your strokes can utilize either the power stroke or the rebound stroke, as shown in Lesson 1, and can start and end at the same position ("Stop Where You Start").

- **Full strokes** start approximately 18 inches above the playing surface (18 inches back to 18 inches).
- **Half strokes** start approximately 9 inches above the playing surface (9 inches back to 9 inches).
- **Tap strokes** start approximately 3 inches above the playing surface (3 inches back to 3 inches).
- **Controlled strokes** (downstrokes and upstrokes) start at one level and end at a different level:

    1. **Downstrokes** start from a higher level and stop at a lower level (18 inches to 9 inches, 18 inches to 3 inches, or 9 inches to 3 inches).
    2. **Upstrokes** start from a lower level and rise to a higher level (9 inches to 18 inches, 3 inches to 18 inches, or 3 inches to 9 inches).

Within the Level System, Stone developed a method of using upstrokes to downstrokes and tap strokes so the sticks would be in the proper position in order to 1) produce accents and other dynamics and 2) play the upcoming note(s). This system further allows for control of the drumsticks and the execution of difficult passages. Even though it's normal to use the full and half strokes to produce accents, Stone would have his students practice accents from the tap position as well. This helps build power and velocity. Try playing dynamics (Lesson 4) and finger exercises (Lessons 22 and 23), as well as random accents from the tap position.

The various strokes are notated as follows:

D or ↓ = downstroke

U or ↑ = upstroke

T = tap stroke

F = full stroke

> = accent

Here are a few examples.

Downstroke – Upstroke – Tap Stroke

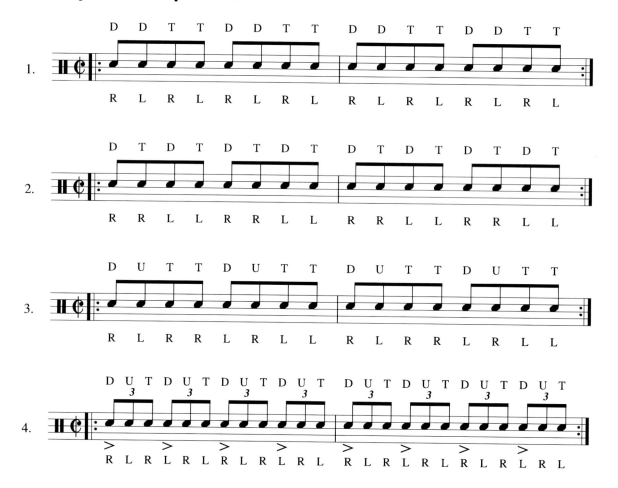

NOTE: Over the years, Stone evolved his teaching methods. His earlier teaching consisted of notating every note in every exercise in *Stick Control* with a mark indicating an upcoming accent, as well as the position the stick must reach in order to properly execute the upcoming note. He made sure his students marked their *Stick Control* books appropriately, as this was part of their homework. Later, his focus turned to marking only those notes where a **U** or up arrow (↑) was needed. This was mainly called for when playing flams and paradiddles (see examples on the next page). In the case of flams, the student would look at the note before each flam.

If a left sticking was played just before a left flam (or a right sticking before a right flam), then the note before the flam would be upstroked. Conversely, if a left sticking was played just before a right flam (or a right sticking before a left flam), then the note before the flam would be downstroked. Check out the examples on the next page.

NOTE: **F** = right flam   (**F**) = left flam

Right and Left Flams

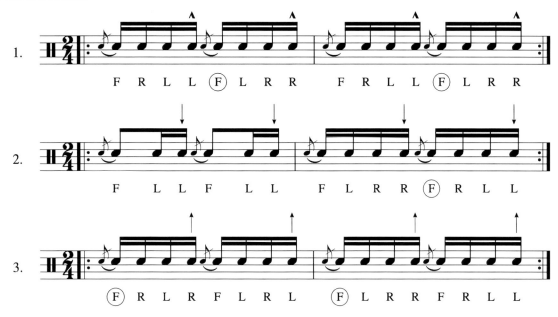

And, in the Case of Paradiddles...

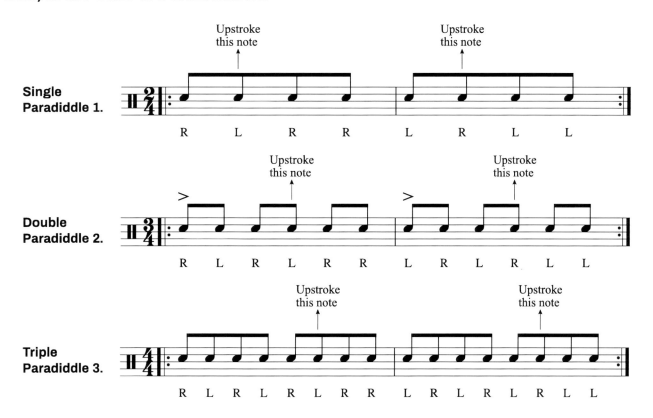

He reasoned that with proper study and execution of the exercises in *Stick Control*, the sticks would naturally downstroke and tap properly. In fact, Stone referred to his Level System as "stick positions," and the downstroke, upstroke, and taps as "stick levels." He was more interested in bringing the stick immediately "Up" (to either the full, half, or tap positions) in one, continuous motion. He would encourage students to practice by starting with one stick held horizontally in either a full, half, or tap position. Next, he would have them raise the other stick until it touched the bottom of the horizontal stick. This was followed by a downstroke to strike the drum surface, followed by a swift

upstroke (via rebound or power stroke) to and hitting the underside of the horizontal stick. As part of your warm-up routine, he always had you practice this motion with both hands many times. Stone described this motion as "Stop Where You Start."

Barry James: It will help the student attain greater control of the sticks if they take the time to study the Level System in depth. There are books and online lessons available detailing the Level System. In my research of Stone's teaching, I didn't find any articles he published on this subject.

LESSON 1. **HANDHOLDS AND STROKES**

Many earnest students/drummers seeking more drumstick speed and control wonder why after weeks of practice, *nothing has happened.*

One hindrance to their expected progress could be careless handholding—not only how the sticks are held but *where.* A handhold by itself may be ideal, but if it is not applied at or near the normal drumstick **fulcrum**—the balancing point, the area from which a stick may be wielded to best advantage—lack of control will ensue.

Fulcrums can be located in different spots to suit the purpose of various devices. For instance, the sketch of the seesaw below shows its fulcrum to be in the exact center of the plank. Here we have a perfect counterbalance, with the weight on one side balancing that of the other.

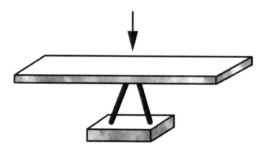

Figure 1.1. Seesaw Fulcrum Point

In contrast, the normal fulcrum of a drumstick is located at some distance, from its center, as shown below, approximately 1 inch towards the butt end of the stick. With this fulcrum, the **over-hang** at the stick's striking end (with its preponderance of weight), gives the stick a maximum balance and response to the slightest movement of the hand. Alternatively, if the stick is held at or near its center (seesaw fulcrum), balance and weight are lost, and the hand alone is left to do most of the work. As a result, the handhold for the weaker (left) hand using the traditional grip is actually more effective when the stick is held in the web of the left hand closer to the seesaw balance point.

Figure 1.2 approximates the location of the fulcrum point of a typical drumstick. About an inch back from the fulcrum is the point at which the stick will balance or "hang" best.

Figure 1.2. Normal Drumstick Fulcrum Point

Find the fulcrum (balance point) of the stick, then come back an inch towards the butt end, and mark the grip point with a permanent marker.

Figure 1.3. Finding the Fulcrum

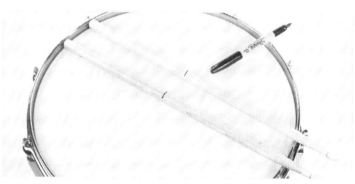

Figure 1.4. Marking the Grip Points

Holding the stick at the grip point (**Figure 1.3**) will afford the stick maximum response to the slightest movement of the hand.

Attention to this little detail in handholding could be the answer to further speed and control.

Check your own handholds against the photos on these pages and compare, first, by holding the stick at the normal balance point, then by coming back towards the butt end of the stick (approximately 1 inch), and finally by closing your thumb and the first crease of your first finger around the stick. This is the principal grip point. Again, I recommend you mark the grip point with a permanent marker.

For an average hand, the butt of the right stick (held normally) should protrude approximately 1 to 1.5 inches from the backside of the hand. The left-stick fulcrum is, of course, the same as the right's. However, owing to the difference in the traditional left handhold, the butt of the left stick will extend 3 to 4 inches from its resting place in the socket of the left thumb and the base of the forefinger.

Start by dropping your hands to your sides. Relax your shoulders, arms, wrists, hands, and fingers. Next, from your elbows, bring your lower arms up so they are parallel to the floor and above the height of the drum.

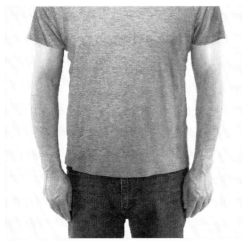 

Figure 1.5. Proper Body Position for Gripping   Figure 1.6. Proper Hand Position for Gripping

Figure 1.7 depicts the hands being held in what is called the **German grip**, in which the top of the hands are showing. The motion is similar to waving goodbye. Note how hand drummers (i.e., conga players) play in this manner.

Figure 1.8 depicts the hands being held using the **French grip.** The motion is similar to using a karate chop, where the thumbs are on top.

 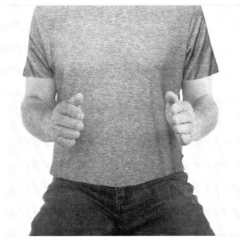

Figure 1.7. German Grip   Figure 1.8. French Grip

Note the space between the thumbs and the first fingers on each hand. Avoid closing the thumbs too tight with the first finger, as this will create tension. The "space" will help relax your hands (see Figure 1.23 on page 16).

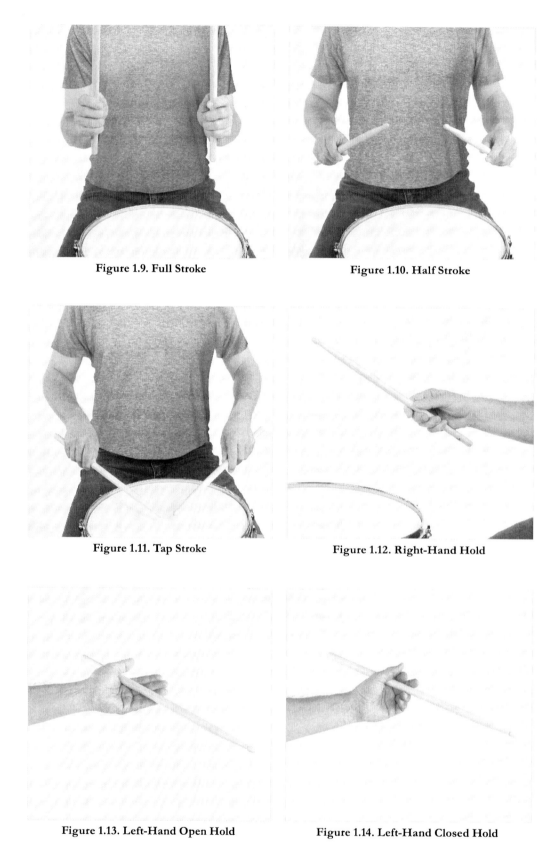

Figure 1.9. Full Stroke

Figure 1.10. Half Stroke

Figure 1.11. Tap Stroke

Figure 1.12. Right-Hand Hold

Figure 1.13. Left-Hand Open Hold

Figure 1.14. Left-Hand Closed Hold

NOTE: When using traditional grip, many drummers use the balance point of the stick as their grip point.

The Educated Thumb Versus the Educated Hand

I often get the following question: "What about this so-called thumb control in the left handhold; the educated thumb, with first and second fingers up in the air. I am told this facilitates control of the drumstick and, hence, better rebounds. Is this something new?"

To me, the only thing new about it is the name **educated thumb.** Through the years, drummers have tried to handle their left drumstick in the easiest way, which, to new players, seems to be by clamping the thumb over the stick as shown in **Figure 1.15**, and letting the first and second fingers idly flap in the breeze. This is more widely known as the **rabbit-ear handhold**. It is, on the face of it, an uncompleted hold. Now, let's compare the difference between **Figure 1.15** and the closed-in hold shown in **Figure 1.16**. You can see that the thumb is now reinforced by the first finger curling around and over the stick, ready to bear down at the discretion of the player. It is further reinforced by the second finger, not by actual contact with the stick, but by its alignment alongside the first.

Let's refer to the hold in **Figure 1.16** as that of the **educated hand**, in which the hand, thumb, and fingers work in unison to wield the stick. This is just another example of a variation in handholding from the one shown in **Figure 1.15**. However, for any hand, the rabbit-ear hold is a weak one and not conducive to maximum control of the left stick. Its use is barred in many rudimental drumming contests as an incomplete hold, and is subject to a markdown by the judges. The use of the finger-bounce technique in modern progressive jazz, in which the action of the left forefinger tapping against the stick plays a most important part, is so well known to the modern drummer that an explanation here seems unnecessary. But, suffice it to say, without the forefinger trained to curl over the left stick (the right fingers have their duty to perform, too), the achievement of a finger bounce is impossible.

Figure 1.15. The Educated Thumb

Figure 1.16. The Educated Hand

Rebound Strokes

Use a fluid motion throughout.

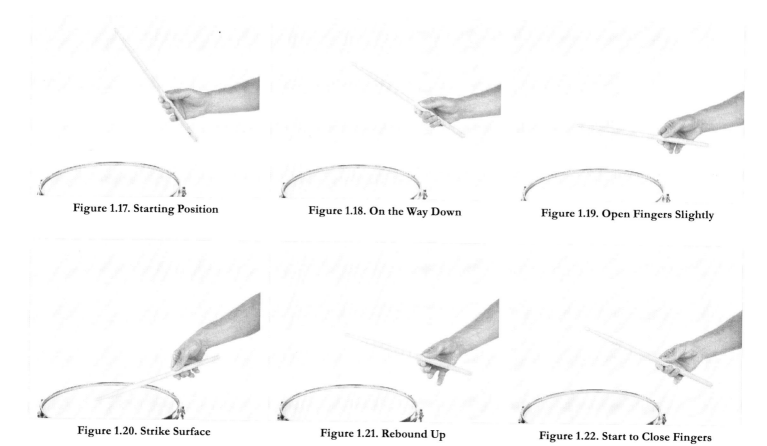

Figure 1.17. Starting Position

Figure 1.18. On the Way Down

Figure 1.19. Open Fingers Slightly

Figure 1.20. Strike Surface

Figure 1.21. Rebound Up

Figure 1.22. Start to Close Fingers

Figure 1.23. Close the fingers at the top of the stroke, and then pull the stick into the palm of your hand.

Figure 1.24. In order to avoid stress and play with a natural grip, be sure to leave a space between your thumb and first finger.

The Carbon Paper Checkup

(Yes, carbon paper can still be purchased at your local office supply store.)

Over the years I've used a simple method to illustrate the contrast among single, double, and the more modern buzz rolls. Many times, this checkup has revealed minor variations in other figures as well that are more easily seen than heard by a student and, consequently, more quickly remedied. However, I find on the carbon that the fill-in beats of the buzz vary considerably in power; the carbon paper shows a ragged continuation of strokes that wouldn't be expected in a smooth-sounding roll, which is often described as resembling "the gentler patter of raindrops on a tin roof." The following is a carbon reproduction of the buzz roll.

The carbon paper method of reproducing drumbeats has long been a part of teaching. It is a simple device for giving a pupil a visual representation of a rudiment or figure that has been played often. This visualization helps to develop listening skills that haven't sufficiently been trained yet to function alone.

The carbon paper checkup is simple to operate. Lay a sheet of white paper on a desk or tabletop, and place a sheet of carbon paper (such as those formally used by typists in making duplicates of letters) inked-side down. Upon this, put a pair of drumsticks into your pupil's hands, and they are ready to go.

Direct the student to execute a rudiment or roll on the carbon. Lift the carbon off, and there it is—their drumming signature appears on the paper before them!

Figure 1.25. Carbon Reproduction of a Buzz Roll

The Power Stroke (A Variation on the Free or Rebound Stroke) by Joe Morello

This technique begins in the full-stroke position, as the wrist can only produce so much power. Therefore, the power stroke will produce a higher level of strength by using the larger muscles in the elbow (focus on the elbow). The wrist does not generate the stroke—the elbow does. From the full-stroke position, the elbow is thrown out (away from the body). At the same time, the tip of the stick moves down toward the drum. The elbow begins the motion, and the wrist follows. The stick then follows and reacts to the motion of the wrist. As the elbow relaxes and returns to the rest position, the wrist reacts back to the full-stroke position. This stroke happens within one second—a flash of power. Because the elbow and biceps are involved behind the stroke, a greater amount of power is produced. This is not the kind of stroke you will use often,

but it is an important reflex exercise so when power is needed, and the stick is at full height, you are prepared to use the correct muscles and technique to produce the best expression. The power stroke is an excellent callisthenic exercise. As a performance stroke, it is useful when playing several consecutive hand-to-hand accents. It is similar to what is referred to as reflex awareness in martial arts, as it helps in making fast movement decisions. This type of reflex action is very important in the modern drumset movement. Use pages 5, 6, and 7 of *Stick Control* to practice the power stroke. Set the metronome at a very slow tempo in order to return to the starting position between each stroke. It will help strengthen larger muscles. Find your own metronome marking to focus and sharpen this movement. Begin in full-stroke position.

The Power Stroke

1. **2.** **3.** **4.**

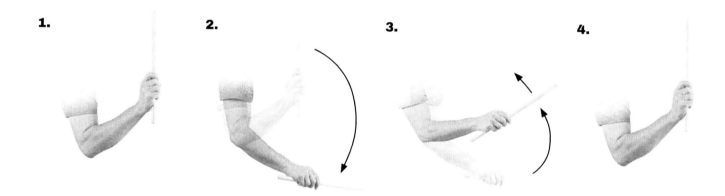

Elbow generates the stroke.
Elbow is thrown out.
Wrist reacts to motion.
Stick hits pad.
Elbow returns to relaxed position.
End in full-stroke position.
Relax.
Concentrate.

LESSON 2. WHAT IS A RUDIMENT?

A **rudiment,** the dictionary tells us, is a first principle; a beginning; that from which something more complex may be developed; something that must be taken, learned, or studied as a foundation for further advance.

Thus, it follows that any figure that can be practiced on a drum may be considered a rudiment. Such rudiments are found in just about any drum method today: C. E. Gardner, Charles Wilcoxon, Vincent L. Mott, you name it. *Stick Control* contains (if you mix and match them) over a thousand rudiments for practice.

The Standard Rudiments

In drumming, we start with the "standard drum rudiments." There is nothing formidable about them. They are simply the first elementary exercises of the drum:

a progressive set corresponding, say, to the first scales and exercises of other instruments. They do not, by any means, represent all a drummer has to know, any more than the same number of scales mastered by a budding pianist will turn them into a finished performer. But they are basic rudiments, first, because they represent, I'm sure most serious teachers will agree, the logical place to begin.

NOTE: The original 26 rudiments introduced by NARD (National Association of Rudimental Drummers) were increased to 40 rudiments by PAS (Percussive Arts Society). Also, the 26 standard rudiments shown below were originally written in the bass clef. Modern transcriptions of these and other drum parts are now written in the neutral (sometimes referred to as percussion or rhythm) clef, as shown below.

The Original Standard 26 American Drum Rudiments

8. The Drag or Half Drag

9. The Single Drag or Single Drag Tap

10. The Double Drag or Double Drag Tap

11. The Single Paradiddle

12. The Double Paradiddle

13. The Flam Paradiddle

14. The Flam Paradiddle-Diddle

15. The Drag Paradiddle #1

16. The Drag Paradiddle #2

17. The Single Ratamacue

18. The Double Ratamacue

19. The Triple Ratamacue

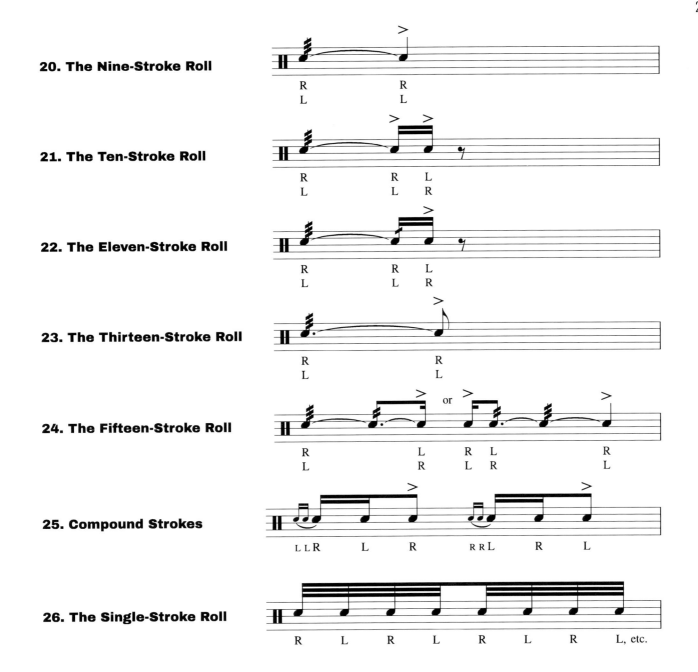

20. The Nine-Stroke Roll

21. The Ten-Stroke Roll

22. The Eleven-Stroke Roll

23. The Thirteen-Stroke Roll

24. The Fifteen-Stroke Roll

25. Compound Strokes

26. The Single-Stroke Roll

In many musical examples, the above 26 rudiments may be found written with altered accents and rhythms to enhance the artistry of a particular composer's work; however, the examples will still be drawn from the rudiments above. When performing isolated rudiments, as in an audition or a contest, it is common practice for the chosen rudiment to be played from slow to fast to slow using gradual *accelerandos* and *decelerandos* followed by the opposite to bring the rudiment to a close.

Example 2.1. The Single Paradiddle

22

In addition to the 26 standard American drum rudiments practiced during the "Stone" era, there are now a total of 40 rudiments adopted by the Percussive Arts Society. Here are the additional 14 rudiments.

The Additional 14 Rudiments

27. The Single-Stroke Four

RLRL RLRL
LRLR LRLR

28. The Single-Stroke Seven

RLRLRLR
LRLRLRL

29. The Triple-Stroke Roll

RRRLLLRRRLLL

30. The Multiple-Bounce Roll

31. The Six-Stroke Roll
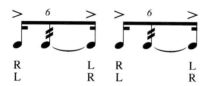

R L R L
L R L R

32. The Seventeen-Stroke Roll

R R L L

33. The Triple Paradiddle

RLRLRLRRLRLRLRLL

34. The Single Paradiddle-Diddle

RLRRLLRLRRLL
LRLLRRLRLLRR

35. The Single Flammed Mill

L R R L RrL L R L

36. Pataflafla

L R L RrLLR L RrL

37. Swiss Army Triplet
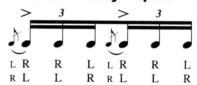

L R R L L R R L
R L L R r L L R

38. Inverted Flam Tap

L R LrL R L R LrL R

39. Flam Drag

L R LLRrL R R L

40. Single Dragadiddle

RR L R R LL R L L

Future Rudiments

At first there were 13 rudiments, then 26, and now 40. How about 52 or 1,052? I'm sure that will eventually be the case. You see, these rhythms of ours have no boundaries. They are infinite. As long as there are creative musicians pushing the outer limits of rhythmic exploration, we will continue to see great changes in drumming. With further developments in television and computers, we will encounter the development of "world rhythms" merging with our American rhythms. What an exciting future for our brotherhood of drummers.

How will these new rudiments be constructed? Most likely starting from the rudiments we currently have.

Today our rudiments are broken down into four categories: roll rudiments, diddle rudiments, flam rudiments, and drag rudiments.

I believe future rudiments will fuse two or more of these categories to form a hybrid sort of rudiment. They will be discovered when our Curious George is in need of *the sound of two or more rudiments meeting—in order to satisfy a particular musical phrase.*

Let's take a look at some of these possibilities.

Future Rudiments

You get the idea. Now, put on your creative caps, and invent your own future rudiments.

LESSON 3. **THE METRONOME**

As a timekeeper, the **metronome** is an invaluable aid to the practicing drummer, as it marks the time at any speed at which it is set. Its clocklike action enables a player to play rhythmic figures along with it *in time,* slow or fast, hot or cold. Here it could well be called a *measuring stick.*

The use of a metronome enables the drummer, who conceives solos and breaks for instance, to execute them not only at his or her desired tempo but at any tempo. This is important because many students fall into the habit of working up their solos at one tempo—usually the one most playable for them. Their hands don't work as well at the tempos they think, and so the practice of solos timed by the metronome (sometimes set slower, sometimes faster), helps to impart the flexibility needed to streamline the drumbeats into the beat of any band, or at any tempo.

For students interested in gaining speed, the metronome is a *must.* This person makes a practice of working on exercises to develop speed until, as Joe Morello puts it, "it hurts." At that point, or later, they check their efforts against the metronome and, when they find they have advanced their speed another notch and can still hang on, they are, for the moment, *a most happy person.*

If, in the endeavor to reach an extra notch, the student practices so hard, so fast, or so long that they become tangled up into a mental knot and physical tension, all they have to do is slow down the good old timekeeper a few notches, relax at the slower tempos, and begin the upward climb again.

The one thing to try and avoid is the excessive use of this instrument—as timekeeper, that is. One shouldn't depend on it to the extent that accurate timing cannot be maintained without it. Thus, used sparingly, the metronome can be "a good tool." If used too much, it can become "a distraction while trying to establish your inner clock."

Joe Morello's Thoughts on the Use of a Metronome

I feel that the exercises in any book should be practiced with a metronome. But it is important to understand what a metronome will do and what it will not do.

A metronome will help you to be rhythmically accurate; it will not teach you to swing. The metronome can be used to gauge your development; it should not be used as a challenge. Let's look at each of these points.

The metronome is useful in helping you to space your notes correctly and keep time. The metronome will not slow down when you play the fast parts; it won't speed up on the slow parts; it won't change the pulse when you change from eighths to triplets to sixteenths. It can be very valuable

in helping you learn rhythmic relationships (such as those in the "Table of Time" from my book *Master Studies*). It will also help prepare you for playing with a click track, something you'll encounter in a recording studio.

The metronome will not teach you to swing or groove. That has to do with feeling, and the metronome has no feeling; it's a machine. However, don't be afraid of the metronome either. There has been a myth going around for years that if you practice with a metronome, you'll play mechanically. That's not true. So, use the metronome as a guide, but don't let it become more important than it really is.

One way of using it as a guide is by gauging your progress with it. As your proficiency increases, you can play with the metronome set at higher tempos. Psychologically, being able to see your progress is helpful. But, don't get involved in a speed contest with the metronome. When you forget about being musical and start worrying about speed, you are defeating the purpose of the music. Being able to play sixteenth notes at a metronome setting of 270 bpm doesn't mean a thing if you can't play them musically.

I suggest starting off slowly each time you practice and making sure you are totally relaxed. After your muscles are warmed up, you can gradually increase the tempo, one metronome marking at a time. If, at any point, you start to feel tension in your hands, wrists, or arms, *stop.* Move the metronome back a couple of notches, and work from a tempo at which you are totally relaxed. This is what will eventually build speed.

We all have days when we don't seem to be able to play as well. Maybe yesterday you were able to play a certain exercise with the metronome set at 160, but today you feel tension if you try to go past 148. Fine, stay at 148. Playing stiffly at 160 won't do you a bit of good. Your top speed may go up and down from day to day, but if you take an average of your speed and compare it from week to week, you should see some improvement.

Experiment using the metronome on different beats, starting with a click on each beat of the bar. After you feel comfortable with that, change the click to just the first beat of each bar, then to beats 2 and 4 of each bar, followed by the "and" of each bar. There are a variety of ways to use the metronome, so use your imagination.

From Barry James: There are many professional drum teachers who have expressed concern over the use of the metronome/click track. It is possible for a student to become dependent on the regular "clicks" or "beeps" from this robotic timekeeper. As a result, the student may have difficulty developing their own "inner clock." Therefore, it's important to work both with and without a metronome.

LESSON 4. **THAT LIGHT TOUCH ON THE DRUMHEAD**

The ability to lay a pair of sticks down onto a drumhead at lightning speed, combined with accuracy and endurance at a whisper-softness, is supposed to be a "gift" possessed by a few of the favored ones in the upper echelons of the art of drumming. I'll go further and say that this ability definitely *is not* a gift that few possess.

The reason is simple and not based on some "God-given gift." The problem is that not many of those practicing are far-seeing or willing enough to devote a portion of their daily practice period to the development of beats in which volume is toned down to a whisper, and other dynamics become an essential part of the would-be drummers' daily practice.

The average student has a pair of lusty arms just aching to bang those sticks down onto the drumhead (or any striking surface) at breakneck speed, with all the power they can muster. They are speed crazy and have no interest in the many nuances of light and shade. To quote an older teacher, to them the dynamic marking *pp* means *pretty powerful.*

To be sure, speed and power are a *must* in many types of playing encountered. But these two elements fall far short of representing the sum total of the technical equipment required by the modern drummer—*musician*-drummer that is. There are innumerable instances in which the modern drummer is required to play their part with the same finesse and skill as that of the other players. This can only be acquired through adequate preparation, not alone on the practice pad, but on the drumhead itself.

The opening two bars of *Bolero*, by Maurice Ravel, demonstrate a pertinent example of dynamic control. Here the whisper/softness is exemplified in this two-bar figure, which, except for the final measures of this piece, is repeated from beginning to end.

The chief feature of *Bolero* is the constant, incessant *crescendo* of the drum from *pp* to the loudest *ff* the player can manage. And, since the duration of the piece is almost 10 minutes long, a terrific amount of concentration is involved in being able to maintain an even graduation of *crescendo* throughout.

Example 4.1. Crescendo in *Bolero* Drum Part

Here are some exercises to help you achieve "dynamic excellence."

Dynamic Excellence Exercises

The following exercises are designed to make the player bring out the marked contrast between notes of one power and those of another. Incidentally, an occasional 15-minute workout on the snare drum itself of just rolling—softer, still softer—and still softer— will work wonders in developing a controlled roll of "whisper power."

For Dynamics—*Fortissimo* to *Pianissimo*

LESSON 5. YOU NEED A PROFESSIONAL DRUM TEACHER

I receive countless letters from young hopefuls who fondly believe that all they have to do in order to become a big-time drummer is to buy a set of drums.

Don't let anyone kid you into thinking that you can become a capable drummer all by yourself. The "do it yourself" artist may be able to build a bookcase or a lawn settee from a set of printed directions, but students need to be trained by experts in how to play a musical instrument in a professional manner.

Yes, you or anyone else can pick up pointers in modern drumming from listening to records or watching performers on videos, YouTube, etc. But, of course, if this process is going to be helpful in any way, it must be based on some sort of an underlying foundation, both musically and manually. How can you expect to imitate sounds and reproduce figures you've heard without capable *and intelligent* hands to guide the drumsticks or brushes over your practice pad or drumset?

Joe Morello once stated, "It is true that today's jazz man does his best work when inspired and that inspirational style must come from *feeling*, that *something*, which one either has or has not."

"But," he added, "It is equally true that those so-called heaven-sent messages that often come to the soloist while playing on the set are beyond his/her reach if they haven't the well-trained and coordinated hands to lay them down upon a set of skins and cymbals." The bottom line—find a professional percussion teacher, and take as many lessons as you can.

The professional drum teacher should be a person who has had some years of experience performing on, as well as teaching, percussion instruments. He or she should be well grounded in the rudiments, be able to read musical notation, and be able to teach all styles of music.

LESSON 6. ROLLS IN GENERAL (ATTACK AND RELEASE)

The precise instant in which to play a roll (the drummer's long tone) to match the long notes played in an ensemble of other instruments, is a simple matter. It's in the drum part right in front of you, and somewhere in the offering is the conductor giving you the beat with a baton. Therefore, you can't miss an attack. Or, let's put it this way: you *shouldn't*.

The release of a roll is another matter and not so clearly indicated, if indicated at all. Furthermore, the drummer has a problem all their own, for while a wind player affects a release by just ceasing to blow and a string player by lifting the bow, the drummer is challenged with playing thirty-second notes by which they've been taught to produce said roll.

The simplest method of explaining the release of untied rolls to the elementary pupil is through the mathematical breakdown of the rolls to thirty-second notes. This is standard procedure in demonstrating roll values to the beginner.

At the normal playing tempo that the instructor has carefully selected for demonstration, the pupil finds they can "roll with the music"—that the normal speed of hand alternation when rolling synchronizes with the playing tempo. Thus, the student will find themselves actually playing a passable roll using the exact number of thirty-second notes indicated by the three-line abbreviation shown against the whole note directly below.

Example 6.1. Roll with the Music

Release by Yardstick

Now, using the thirty-second note formula, a rolled whole note played at a fast tempo is, or can be, ended with a single tap (a light one) on its final quarter note.

Example 6.2. Ending on a Quarter Tap

At a medium tempo, the roll can be ended similarly on its final eighth note.

Example 6.3. Ending on an Eighth Tap

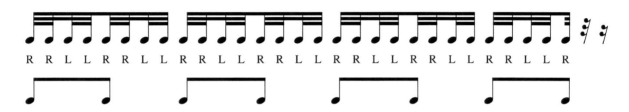

Or, at a slow tempo on its final sixteenth note.

Example 6.4. Ending on a Sixteenth Tap

The release in the uncounted roll can be accomplished by simultaneously lifting both sticks from the drumhead within the same timeframe shown above.

Rolling with the Music

Rolling in rhythm, when it can be done, is an accepted method for rolling when you're playing in an ensemble. It is especially effective in a simple binary measure, where it helps us keep time and makes for an easy, effortless flow of hand alternation. But, more often than not, we find we cannot roll in rhythm because the playing tempo is too slow, too fast, or too varied for us to follow. In such instances we throw the thirty-second notes out the window and play an **uncounted or unmeasured roll**, irrespective of the number of beats involved.

This is the finished roll of the expert, who must be prepared to roll *in* rhythm or *against* it at will, as well as be able to shift gears freely and unconsciously from one to the other.

The Counted Roll Versus the Uncounted Roll

Here are some exercises that focus on the flexibility of the *uncounted* roll (in which hand movements are often made against the rhythm), as opposed to the inflexibility of the *counted* roll (in which the hands invariably move with the rhythm). You might ask, "Do you have any special exercises for further development of the free and easy application of the uncounted roll?"

The suggestions I make in this lesson should put you on the right track, but, for additional exercises for everyday practice, try the following examples, in which uninhibited hand motion in rolling is indicated, either with the beat (preferably), or against it at various tempos.

Example 6.5. Counted Versus Uncounted Rolls

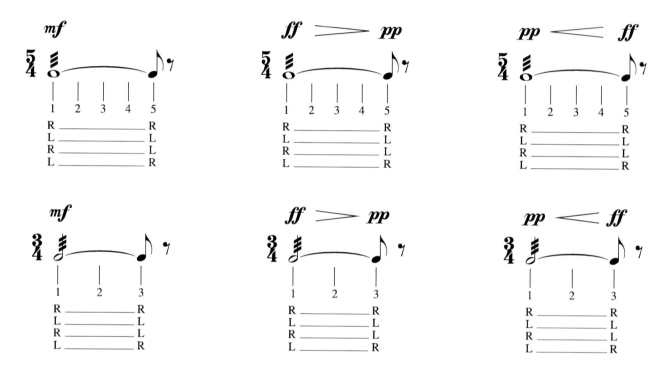

The best method for achieving the desired results with rolling is through the use of a metronome. The second best option is by utilizing foot taps on the floor or on a foot pedal. Practice on the pad is suggested in the beginning, but this must be followed by plenty of work on the drum itself.

Begin by setting the metronome at any given speed. (It doesn't matter what speed.) Poise your sticks, and start the roll on tick number 1. Count the ticks aloud, and end precisely with the proper stick on count 5 or 3, as the case

may be. Repeat each exercise many times before moving on to the next one.

Use a smooth, even roll (sometimes in a two-beat style, sometimes with a buzz), and don't, at any time, try to match the timing of your hands to that of the sticks. This will help develop your ability to roll with perfect freedom—*with* the beat when you can, and against the beat when you can't.

Try the next four examples broken down as buzz-roll hand movements, and then as double-stroke roll hand movements.

Example 6.6. Buzz Versus Double-Stroke Rolls

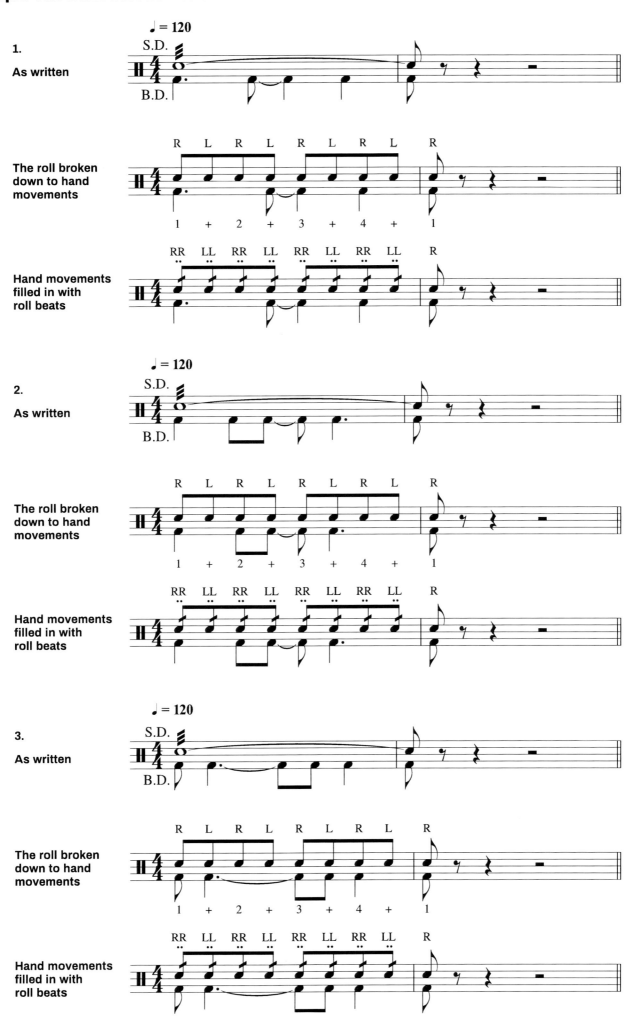

32

Rolls broken out, continued.

One for the Eager Beaver

Notice that the sixteenth-note rolls in the exercises above start with a single stroke that is followed by double strokes. This is an excellent way to help insure that the secondary stroke will be of equal volume with the primary stroke.

LESSON 7. **FLEXIBILITY IN ROLLING**

The conscientious professional will find it expedient to pause occasionally in their mad career to review their fundamental technique, "looking for trouble." They will not have far to look. Hardly will they get their sticks comfortably into their hands before finding themselves bumping up against the *long roll,* the drummer's long tone—onc of the first lessons essayed as a beginner, and one of the last to be perfected by the expert.

There are so many methods available for practicing long and short rolls. Because of their many ramifications, it would take an entire book to do the subject justice. But, our trouble-seeking friend will find that one method of value lies in being able to study the coordination of hand action in rolling—the timing of the hand movements with (or against) the rhythm of the time signature.

For instance, we find that at a specified tempo we can roll easily "with the rhythm," and, when possible, this is a good thing to do. The chart below shows the possible hand movements (pulsations) involved in executing the same roll pattern at various tempos.

However, when a playing tempo does not lend itself to a comfortably timed pulsation, we need to use an uncounted roll, which requires as many or as few hand movements that will fill the duration of its notated value. And here, flexibility in rolling enters into the picture.

The need for flexibility also occurs when a playing tempo varies, possibly from measure to measure. The following exercises, which are each designed for an unvaried tempo, will aid in rolling *with* or *against* the rhythm at will.

The Flexible Roll

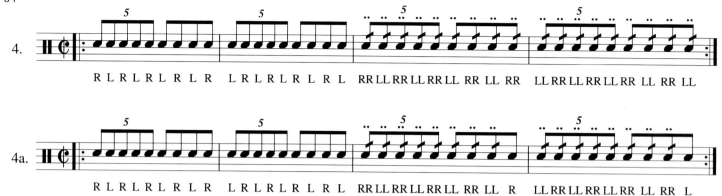

4.

R L R L R L R L R   L R L R L R L R L   RR LL RR LL RR LL RR LL RR   LL RR LL RR LL RR LL RR LL

4a.

R L R L R L R L R   L R L R L R L R L   RR LL RR LL RR LL RR LL R   LL RR LL RR LL RR LL RR L

Now, to Start

Play through the individual measures of the exercise, *No Accents*, below, and repeat each one many times before proceeding to the next. Play at a given, even tempo, not slow to fast. Start slowly at first, then go slightly faster, and so on until you're up to capacity.

Play the exercise with a metronome if you'd like.

You'll notice that accents have not been notated.

No Accents

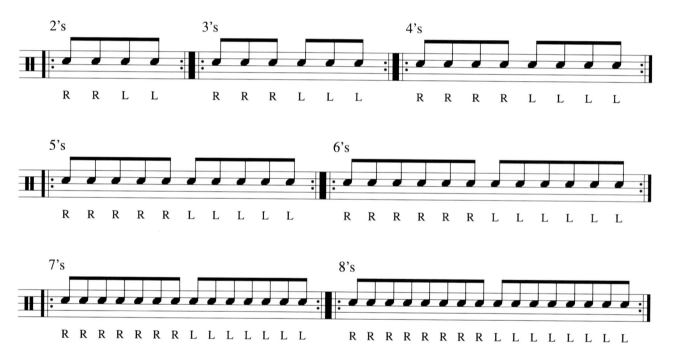

Now, go through the same measures again, this time accenting the first beat of each group. Then play the measures a second time, but accent the last beat of each group. Finally, go through the measures a third time, but accent both the first and last beats of each group.

The following exercise shows the individual measures of *No Accents* combined into a single study with clock-tick regularity. No accents here.

Practicing Consistency with No Accents

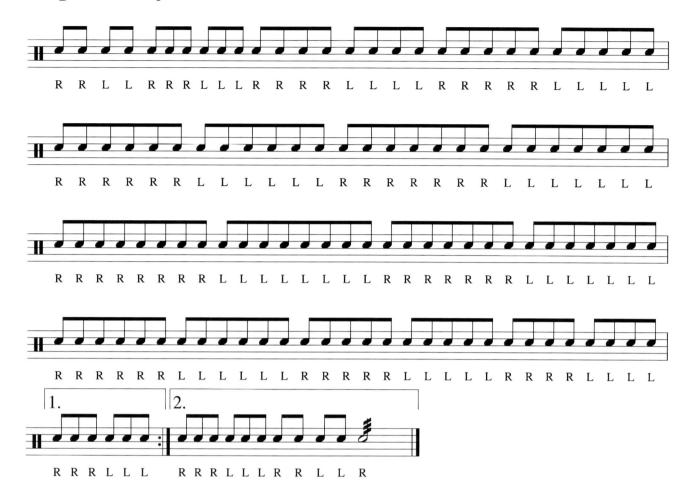

Now, accent the first beat of each group.

Practicing Consistency with First-Beat Accents

And, to finish, accent the last beat of each group.

Practicing Consistency with Last-Beat Accents

LESSON 8. **THE RUFF/DRAG AND BUZZ RUFF**

Some call it a **ruff**; others say **drag**. Since our older authorities (Strube, Bruce, Emmett, etc.) referred to this rudiment as a *ruff*, I will follow in that tradition. However, the way we say it is secondary in importance to the way we play it.

A *ruff* is comprised of a single beat of given power, preceded by two grace notes, and struck by the off stick with less power. It is a comparable figure to our **flam**, which is composed of a similar single beat preceded by a grace note.

Whereas the flam, when played, sounds like its phonetic *flam (f-lam)*, the ruff sounds, when spoken, more like *r-r-uff*, with the rolling r's of the Scotchman. One drummer I know has named it *brrup*, which, with the right inflection, more accurately follows the sound of the rudiment.

Proper execution of the *ruff* at normal playing tempos calls for precise placement of the grace notes. Moeller has said, "… there is the same amount of time between the first and second grace note as there is between the second grace note and the principal note. They are all of equal distance." This, along with the proper balance of power between principal and grace notes, makes for the ideal ruff, which may be executed at slow tempos in **open** style (two struck taps followed by the principal beat) or, at more normal tempos, in a **closed** style (one tap and one rebound followed by the principal beat).

All this leads to the question, "Can the grace notes of the ruff be buzzed?" This is a matter of choice, but there is no reason why on occasion they shouldn't be, for the two grace notes of the ruff, when doubled, are indeed a segment of the long roll itself; it is the shortest member of the roll, or the roll of two beats. Therefore, if our long roll and other short rolls can be (and often are) executed by buzz to achieve finer, smoother rolling, so can our roll of two beats, whether by itself or as a part of the ruff.

Thus we have, if we choose, the **buzz ruff.**

Example 8.1. The Buzz Ruff

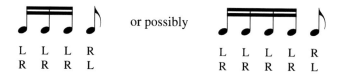

Of course, the buzz ruff has no place in classical music—the works of the masters—in which we are expected to execute the figures in our drum parts as written or, as known by the experienced drummer, as intended. Similarly, the buzz ruff is out of place in military drumming or solo presentation in competition. There the open, two-beat roll is used exclusively.

However, the buzz ruff has its place, giving us an additional tool of our trade, and offering a greater flexibility of expression. With its ad-lib style, it can often be used effectively, for instance, in accentuating some action onstage in a floor show. It can be created with a short, sharp explosive—an exaggerated buzz, crushed down upon the drumhead and ending with a *sfz* rim shot, as shown in example 8.2.

Example 8.2. The Exaggerated Buzz Ruff

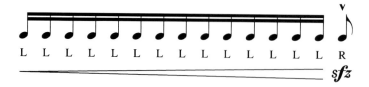

LESSON 9. **THE TWO-BEAT ROLL VERSUS THE BUZZ ROLL**

The two-beat roll is the pure roll and consists of two beats played with either stick: the first beat struck, the second beat rebounded (bounced).

A Beat and Rebound of Either Stick

As the speed increases, it will become necessary to use a different technique in order to close the roll so that both the primary stroke and secondary stroke (bounced) are the same volume.

First, it's important to understand that the double-stroke roll shares the same hand movement as the single-stroke roll. However, by allowing the rebound of the stick to return immediately back to the surface as a second hit, you will achieve a double-stroke roll. (It's a two-for-one special.)

In order to achieve this, it's important to understand that you will be playing at a faster speed than what your wrists alone will be able to handle. And, as you play faster, your hands will naturally be closer to the surface (about 2 to 3

inches above). As you play the primary stroke, allow the stick to rebound up. But, instead of forcing it back down with another stroke, simply pull the butt end of the stick (forcefully) into your hand. This is referred to as either the **throw/pull or push/pull technique**. I suggest the secondary stroke be "forcefully" pulled back into the fleshy part of the palm of your hand. This should provide the accent the secondary stroke needs to balance the volume between the primary and secondary strokes.

Here are a few exercises to help balance the volume and help your double-stroke roll "sing."

Also, check out the etude, *One for the Eager Beaver*, in Lesson 6.

Artificial Accents on the Secondary Strokes

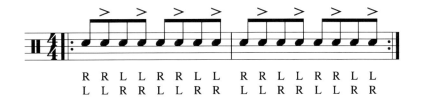

Begin the roll with a single stroke, and then start your doubles (fooling your brain). For more work on your double or rebounded rolls, refer to *Accents and Rebounds*.

More Artificial Accents on the Secondary Strokes

A Buzz of Either Stick

Whereas a slight downward pressure of hands and fingers produces the single rebound of the two-beat roll (above), a further downward pressure will produce two, three, or more rebounds, thus producing the buzz.

A Buzz of Either Stick

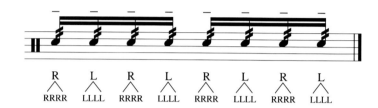

The Two-Beat Roll Versus the Buzz

The buzz roll has always been a controversial subject among drummers, primarily because its character, uses, and limitations have not fully been understood. Prejudice against the buzz roll apparently started in early war times with the inception of military drumming, in which the drummer's duties were confined to outdoor drumming for marching soldiers. The rolls, then employed on a giant parade drum with heavy drumsticks, were powerful in nature, and, in this context, buzzing was definitely out of place. Hence, the drummer of this era was warned against buzzing, and they in turn transmitted this warning to those who followed.

Then and Now

Through the intervening years, new developments in music and in drumming have come into existence one by one. New instruments and playing techniques have been introduced into our percussion section. These, in and of themselves, have called for innovations and new techniques, one of which has been the buzzing of the roll.

Through my many years of teaching, in the magazine articles I've written, and in my clinics, I have endeavored to emphasize the importance of the buzz (sometimes called "press" or "crush") roll and justify its use in today's drumming. Why? Because it is a natural extension of our traditional two-beat roll. And, because it represents an additional tool of the drumming trade, not merely a "good enough" or "get by" device to replace the two-beat.

Roll Versus Sandpaper

Today, the all-around drummer finds use for as many degrees of coarseness and fineness in their rolls as there are in sandpaper, each degree dedicated to its particular purpose and type of drum. While it is agreed that the pure two-beat roll comes first in rudimental importance (and is still the preferred roll of the stylist), modern drumming, especially on a small wire-snared drum played with lightweight sticks, more often calls for a finer, smoother roll, aptly said to resemble the "patter of raindrops on a tin roof" or the "tearing of a piece of silk cloth."

Wire snares buzz by themselves at the slightest sound disturbance or the single tap of a stick. And, they can often buzz as a result of certain tones played on some nearby instrument. Therefore, it is difficult for the player, even while attempting a two-beat roll on the sensitive wire-snared drum, to achieve anything but a buzz, since the snares move faster than the sticks.

"Avoiding the Buzz" Is for the Beginner

Yes, there are many fine teachers who tell their students to avoid the buzz. This writer also believes the admonition to be a good one, but such a warning is primarily intended for practice and, particularly, for the beginner, so they may be trained to master the more difficult but generally accepted two-beat roll first.

Later, as training and experience help develop the skills of the beginner (or anyone seeking more proficiency), they will find control of their rolls developing alongside them. The ultimate objective is to be able to apply them in their many gradations of tone, from the *pianissimo* of the fine buzz on the smaller drum, to the *fortissimo* roar of the two-beat played on the gut-snared military drum.

It is here, within the sound-scope of the roll (the drummer's long tone), that the buzz occupies its highly important place.

LESSON 10. **SIGHT-READING**

Sight-reading rests in the ability to read note groups quickly and accurately, while at the same time selecting the stick that's best suited for the execution. When properly developed, reading a drum part is as simple as reading a newspaper.

One of the elements of sight-reading is eye fixation. The eyes take in note groups only when they pause and fix in their travel across the page. The speed of a drummer's eye-travel determines the speed of their tempo. While a beginner may see one note group on each such pause, an expert reader, their eye span widened and skilled through practice, will take in several groups.

Data shows that a highly skilled word reader can read more than 1,400 words a minute and retain what they've read. (At this rate you, the musician reader, should be able to take in and remember this lesson on sight-reading in 20 seconds. Try it and see how good you are.)

It would be interesting to compare the performance of a word reader skimming a clear-cut printed page with that of a drummer confronted with a smudged, moth-eaten manuscript part that came over in the ark, full of penciled cuts, cues, and erasures, *all while watching the leader for sudden stops!* Or, that of a violinist speeding through a work of, say, Stravinsky, and being obliged not only to read the notes but to make the tones as well. Or, that of a pianist reading a flock of notes scored on two staves with additional instructions such as *"transpose it down half a step."* I'm not the one to put down the accomplishments of the other type of reader, but I truly believe that the sight-reading standards set up by a professional musician, *in their everyday playing*, would be hard for others to meet.

The major difficulty in rapid sight-reading by the drummer is due to the impatience of the average novice who tries to force their eyes and mind to wade through intricate figures at top speed before fully learning to recognize their components, and their note arithmetic. The main difficulty is due to the fact that the student hasn't found time to memorize the relative values of *rests* as thoroughly as those of *notes.*

Rapid sight-reading must be developed through slow, concentrated study in the beginning, and a carefully regulated progress thereafter. The novice will do well to begin by sight-reading one measure, or even one *note group* at each eye fixation, and to assimilate that one before moving on. Soon, with practice, they will be taking in *two, three,* and so on. Even at this point the student is not an expert. Patience is paramount, and forcing (a standard technique later) must be avoided unless reading, interpreting, and execution all suffer in the rush.

Slow sight-reading for the beginner is the appropriate method. I believe that slow, careful study comes first in sight-reading just as slow, elementary control of the drumsticks must be mastered before speedy and precise execution can be achieved. It boils down to starting at the beginning in both departments. This is, of course, if you are dealing with a serious student.

We all have two minds: the conscious and the subconscious. Our conscious mind is the voluntary one; our slow-moving mind is the one with which we study, reason, and think things out. Our subconscious mind is the fast-moving one; it controls our bodily functions and operates from habit and reflex action. If our hand strays too close to a flame, the sensation of heat or pain will be transmitted to our subconscious mind, which, in a split second, by its reflex action, tells our hand to jump away—long before the slower-moving conscious mind has gotten around to figuring out that something is wrong. We jump before we think.

The same principle applies to reading music. The student's first study of a note group must be with their conscious mind. To them, this note group is something new and different. They probably will look at it, compute its arithmetic, see if they are holding their sticks properly, look at it again, and, with everything clearly understood, slowly and carefully play it. (Remember, as I said above, a serious student.) They must do the same thing over and over with this and other groups until they're able to read and play them *automatically.*

Automatically means that through practice, their subconscious mind has finally taken over the job and will now be able to play such note groups without thinking. In other words, when their eyes now light on a well-studied note group, their hands automatically move the sticks through the set of motions their conscious mind has been drilled to associate with that group. In the meantime, their thoughts may be a thousand miles away.

Rapid Sight-Reading Follows

As discussed earlier, one of the elements of rapid sight-reading is **eye fixation**. As sight-reading skills develop, the eyes are able to take in wider groups of notes as they travel across the page. The speed of the reader's eye travel determines the speed of their performance.

With such a slow, concentrated start, and through carefully monitored progress thereafter, the student will eventually find that reading their drum part is as simple and easy as reading a newspaper.

The Key to Good Sight-Reading Is "Counting"

The way to analyze a drum figure is to break it down mathematically to its basic structure. The way to measure structural values is to count aloud while practicing. The oral count is the pupil's anchor—the yardstick by which rhythmic patterns are measured and comprehended. It is the way the student acquires the **rhythmic visualization** needed for playing the patterns. Without it, the student will be working in a vacuum.

The Oral Count in Practice

Regardless of whether a student is sight-reading or simply practicing for next week's lesson, they must count aloud. The tongue is smarter than the hands, in that if a student can be trained to *speak* the subdivisions of a specific figure precisely, they will not have much trouble *playing* them.

Another benefit to counting out loud is that it gives the teacher the advantage of being able to listen so that unevenness and/or slurring of the tongue can be detected.

This is a great way to see if the pupil's *conception* of the rhythm being played is distorted—that is, distorted in the exact ratio to the distortion of the spoken count. To boil it down, *if you can't say it—you can't expect to play it.* When the oral count has finally served its purpose, it may be dropped. We don't need to do as much counting aloud in advanced studies, and we certainly don't need to do it at all in an actual performance. However, in elementary study it is a must and should be continued until it automatically becomes built into the student's technique.

Now, take the suggestions offered in this lesson, place a drum part you haven't played before on your music stand, and "sight-read" it.

Here is an etude in **5/8** time. It is a good piece to count aloud while sight-reading.

Sight-Reading Challenge: Etude in 5/8

LESSON 11. **PRACTICE POINTERS FOR THE BUZZ (MULTIPLE-BOUNCE) ROLL**

Over the years I've answered questions regarding the proper method in which to produce the buzz roll. I've responded that although our Peck's bad boy, the **buzz roll**, is so easily picked up that elementary pupils invariably drift into it like ducks taking to water, an instructor should insist upon the student mastering the rudimental two-beat roll before the buzz. The continuation of this premise is as follows.

After mastering the pure two-beat roll, move on, if you choose, and concentrate on the buzz. The buzz may be applied to a roll executed at any speed at which a roll may be rebounded.

Whereas a single downward pressure of the hands and fingers (as the stick strikes its primary stroke) produces the single rebound of the two-beat roll, a further downward pressure will produce two, three, or several rebounds of the buzz.

Since the buzz is so comparatively easy to execute, one is apt to play it lackadaisically, without paying too much attention to a well-timed hand alternation. As in the two-beat roll, timing of the buzz should be even, whether rolling in or against the rhythm of the music. I have noticed a tendency among pupils, and some professionals as well, to execute their buzz rolls with a slightly faster alternation than with the two-beat variety. This may be, in part, due to the fact that the buzz is easier to produce. Then again, a player may unconsciously hurry his alternation of the buzz for fear of it sounding uneven—with noticeable spaces between the hand strokes.

Break It Down

Here is another challenge in teaching that can most readily be solved by the same type of crude yardstick approach—the mathematical breakdown. To begin with, the figure below is a common one in binary measure, showing rolls *that may be buzzed* matched to single eighth-note beats.

Example 11.1. Mathematical Buzz Roll

NOTE (Barry James): Today's buzz (multiple-bounce) rolls are sometimes notated with a "Z" struck through the stem of the note to be buzzed. In Stone's day, buzz rolls were notated with three strikes going through the stem of the note to be buzzed. There was no distinction (until Stone devised one) among single-stroke, double-stroke, and buzzed rolls. All three types of rolls were notated alike (i.e., with three strikes across the stem of the note(s) to be rolled). Stone also drew a distinction between double-stroke (open) and buzz rolls in his book *Accents and Rebounds* by using "dash" markings (- - - -) over the rolls that were to be buzzed, and "dot" markings (.. .. ..) over those to be double stroked.

If rolled in the rhythm using eighth notes, the buzzes may be broken down to their basic hand-movement pattern as shown on the following page.

Example 11.2. Buzz Roll Hand-Movement Break Out

1	and	2	and	3	and	4	and
Buzz	Buzz	Buzz	Buzz	Buzz	Buzz	Buzz	Buzz
R	L	R	L	R	L	R	L

Practiced at a slow speed, the timing of the single beats and buzzes should follow one another with clocklike regularity. Musically, here is where we cringe, for at a slow tempo our buzzes will sound sad, with great open spaces between them. However, this is how it should be, for at this point the timing is all that matters. When the timing has been brought under control, the speed of the figure may then be advanced. Naturally, the speed of the hand alternation advances correspondingly until, when normal playing tempo is reached, the buzzes have morphed into that smooth, uninterrupted, and un-pulsated long tone of the drum (so aptly defined as "the patter of raindrops on a tin roof").

The following example shows a further matching of the hand movement—that of both the two-beat roll and the buzz, timed by single eighth notes that set up the pattern for either roll.

Two-Beat and Buzz Roll Hand-Movement Break Out

R L R L   R R L L R R L L   R L R L   R L R L

Here is a similar example in **6/8** time.

Exercise 11.5. 6/8 Buzz Roll Hand-Movement Break Out

R L R L R L   R R L L R R L L R R L L   R L R L R L   R L R L R L

On the following page is a rudimental exercise, *Exhibition*, from George Lawrence Stone's book *Military Drum Beats*. Although the rolls in this exercise are designated as five-, seven-, nine-, and thirteen-stroke rolls, the performer has some discretion as to which numbered roll to play (depending on the tempo of the music). For example, a five-stoke roll may be more appropriate at faster tempos, while a seven-stroke roll (played in the manner of a triplet) may be more appropriate at slower tempos.

In rudimental circles, these rolls will usually be performed as double-stroke rolls, though occasionally a single-stroke numbered roll may sneak into the mix. For this lesson, play all the rolls as buzz rolls. Of course, it won't hurt to also play them as singles and doubles just to keep with tradition.

Remember, a five-stroke buzz roll consists of two buzzes and a single stroke, a seven-stroke buzz roll consists of three buzzes and a single stroke, a nine-stroke buzz roll consists of four buzzes and a single stroke, an eleven-stroke buzz roll consists of five buzzes and a single stroke, a thirteen-stroke buzz roll consists of six buzzes and a single stroke, and so on.

Exhibition

LESSON 12. **CRESCENDO USING THE SEVEN-STROKE ROLL**

Here's a way in which to build a strong **crescendo** using the rudimental seven-stroke roll.

Below is the breakdown of the rudimental seven as it traditionally appears.

Example 12.1. Rudimental Seven-Stroke Roll

Below are several exercises designed to help you develop ultimate control of the *crescendo* by gaining initial control of the secondary beats.

Control of the Seven-Stroke Roll

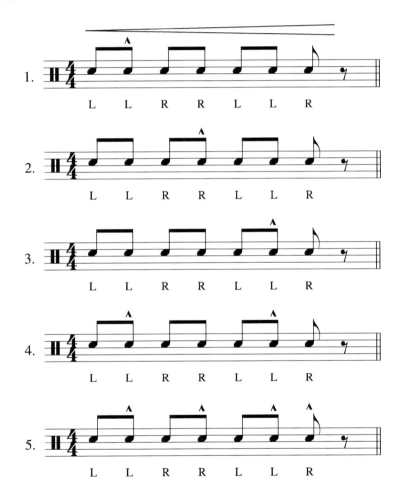

Practice of the *crescendo* in seven is shown in the graph below. I have often found that this graph portrays the note-by-note progression of the *crescendo* more clearly than the formal notation shown at the beginning of this lesson.

L L **R R L L R**

Here is where the most careful attention to stick placement enters the picture. The first beat should be struck from about the 2-inch level, the second from a higher one, the third from an even higher one, and so on, up to the accented seventh. Sticks and hands should rise with the *crescendo*. This follows the same principle as that of the long roll, in which the sticks strike from a lower level to produce a *pianissimo* roll, and from a higher level as the roll increases in power.

LESSON 13. **PARADIDDLES FOR PRACTICE**

Using the three variations of the **paradiddle** and their accents—single (1), double (2), and triple (3)—should help to relieve some of the monotony of practicing them in their basic forms.

First, warm up by playing the individual rudiments slow, to fast, to slow. Now play them together at an even tempo, as shown in the exercises below.

Paradiddle Warm-Up (One of Each)

R L R R L R L R   L L R L R L R L   R R L R L R L R

Repeat ad lib.

Paradiddle Warm-Up (Two of Each)

R L R R L R L L   R L R L R R L R   L R L L R L R L

Repeat ad lib.

Paradiddle Warm-Up (Three of Each)

R L R R L R L L   R L R R L R L R   L L R L R L R R

L R L R L L R L   R L R L R R L R   L R L R L L R L

R L R L R R L R   L R L L R L R L   R R L R L R L L

Repeat ad lib.

LESSON 14. **PLAYING FASTER PARADIDDLES**

The same question, with a different perspective, can be asked regarding the *speedy* execution of paradiddles. After a certain speed and command are reached, there seems to be a tendency to execute the final two beats of each paradiddle as a rebound instead of an original stroke.

Example 14.1. Speedy Single Paradiddles

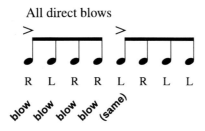

versus

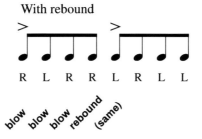

To me, this is generally the wrong approach, as bouncing tends to increase the tempo at the expense of the exact, even spacing of all beats in the execution of this rudiment.

One of my students once told me, "Frankly, I've never gained much speed playing paradiddles. With the rebound question in mind, I've hesitated to practice them seriously, lest I train my hands in the wrong way." Some drummers have told me that maximum speed is achieved only through the rebound. What do you think?

Each Stroke Is a Different Action

George Stone: Of course I think the proper way to execute the paradiddle is by individual hand or finger action for each stroke. This is the manner in which the rudiment

was, and is, intended to be played, and it applies to any paradiddle—single, double, or triple. It is, by the way, the method I recommend for your own practice.

I further think, as most pros do, that the substitution of a rebound for a direct stroke is a makeshift—a shortcut that results in a slurred, uneven sequence of beats that can quite easily degenerate into a triplet figure.

NOTE (Barry James): Try adding an upstroke on the second note of a single paradiddle (on the next page), and watch what happens. You can see that your hands are now in the perfect position to execute the next paradiddle. Likewise, upstroke the fourth note of a double paradiddle and the sixth stroke of a triple paradiddle.

Speeding Up the Paradiddles

Single Paradiddle

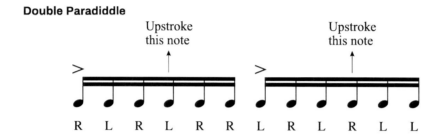

Double Paradiddle

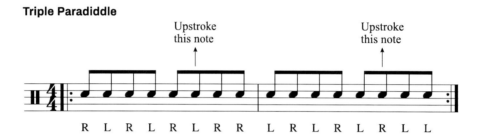

Triple Paradiddle

NOTE (Barry James): If you really want to achieve speed when playing paradiddles, use the upstrokes shown in the exercise above. These upstrokes, as notated, will put your hands in the perfect position to execute the next paradiddle. Try it! Make it your technique each time you play a paradiddle, and watch what happens to your paradiddle chops.

George Lawrence Stone continues: "But, whether we approve or not, the fact remains that the rebound, *only when played in exact rhythm*, is indeed an aid to speed in the paradiddles, and is employed by many pro drummers. And, at real speed, the beats go by so fast it is difficult for the human ear to detect the rebound."

Now, when in due time and with sufficient playing experience under their belt, our hero has mastered speed and continuity to the extent that their hands and fingers move almost by themselves. The rebound in paradiddles, etc., can well creep into the execution *without realizing it* (in exactly the same manner as with the closing of the long roll)! And, I guess, it doesn't take too many words to explain how, at mid-speed between *slow* and *fast*, the stroke and rebound of the faster execution replace the two direct strokes of the slower, without any discernible difference in tone, power, or speed.

On the following page is a set of exercises called *Permutations in Paradiddles,* which I've used with great success in developing control of erratic accentuating. Slow practice is indicated in the beginning, with each exercise repeated many times before moving on to the next. Final practice may be made more interesting and productive by playing exercise 1 for a determined number of times, proceeding without pause to exercise 2, going back without stopping to exercise 1, then going to exercise 3, and so on, throughout the set (exercise 1-exercise 2-exercise 1-exercise 3-exercise 1-exercise 4, etc.). Fifteen minutes on this final version, without stopping, should do the student a lot of good. And, when they sanctimoniously state that they "made" every stroke in their paradiddles *at any speed period!*—tell them they may be right, and steer the conversation into less debatable channels.

Permutations in Paradiddles

Play the following permutations, and then make up some of your own.

For example:

R R L R L L R L L (repeat 20 times)
R L R R L L R L L (repeat 20 times)
L R L L R R L R R (repeat 20 times)
L L R L R R L R R (repeat 20 times)

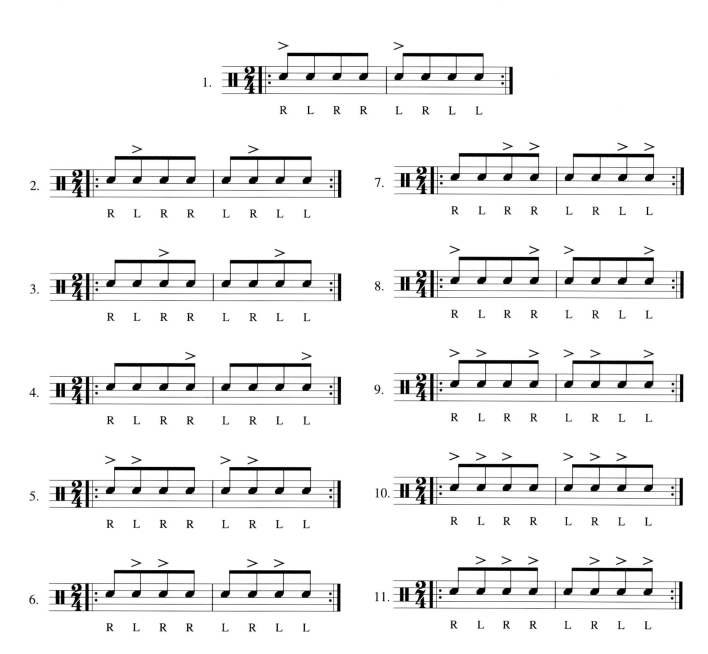

LESSON 15. **FLAMS AND DRAGS (RUFFS)**

A **flam** consists of two single strokes, usually played by alternating sticks at different heights. The first stroke is a quieter grace note, followed by a louder primary stroke with the opposite hand. The two notes are played almost simultaneously, and are intended to sound like a single "fatter" note. In fact, the grace note has no rhythmic value of its own. It is simply an embellishment of the primary stroke.

Example 15.1. Alternated Flams

L R

R L

Compared to a single stroke, the flam produces a thicker and longer-sounding note.

Playing great-sounding flams can be challenging. To do so, it's very important that the grace notes are played as close as possible to the surface of the drum (at the "tap" level). The primary stroke is played higher at either the "half" or "full" level. Playing the grace note at the exact same time as the primary note is called a **flat flam** and has an important place in drumming, particularly in drumset playing, where your hands can strike two different drums at the same time. The idea of the rudimental **alternated flam**, however, calls for the grace note to be played a fraction of a second before the primary note.

It is perfectly acceptable to employ **side (non-alternated) flams** if a high rate of speed prohibits their ideal effect when played alternately.

Example 15.2. Non-Alternated Side Flams

L R   L R   L R   L R   (right-sided)
or: R L   R L   R L   R L   (left-sided)

The Drag (aka The Ruff)

The **drag**, or **ruff** as it is sometimes called, consists of two grace notes before the primary stroke (which is usually accented).

Example 15.3. The Drag

L L R

R R L

Similarly, there are instances in which ruffs "to one side" may be deemed expedient.

Example 15.4. Ruffs to One Side

L L R   L L R   L L R   L L R   (right-sided)
or: R R L   R R L   R R L   R R L   (left-sided)

Grace notes have no rhythmic value on their own, as they are considered an uncounted part of the main note.

The Triple Ratamacue (Traditional Example)

Example 15.5. Non-Alternated Side Drags

LLR LLR LLR L R L RRL RRL RRL R L R

The Flam Tap

The rudimental flam tap is executed in strict rhythm, as written below.

Example 15.6. The Flam Tap

L R   R   R L   L
flam   tap   flam   tap

Of course, there's no reason why the rudiment can't be played as a shuffle rhythm if desired.

Example 15.7. The Shuffle Flam Tap

L R   R R L   L

The flam tap can also be played in a **6/8** time signature, known as Flam Accent #2.

Example 15.8. The 6/8 Flam Tap (aka Flam Accent #2)

L R   R R L   L   L R   R R L   L

But, for rudimental purposes, Example 15.6 illustrates the way it should be played.

LESSON 16. **MORE ON THE FLAM TAP AND FLAM ACCENT**

The Flam Accent (One More Way)

Example 16.1. The Flam Accent

The rudimental flam tap is executed in strict rhythm.

Flam Tap

Example 16.2. The Flam Tap in 2/4

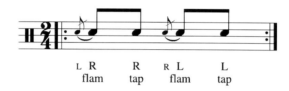

Here are two different ways in which to notate the flam tap in **6/8** time.

Example 16.3. The Flam Tap in 6/8

Example 16.4. Another Flam Tap

Here are some examples showing how flam taps are used in various musical settings.

Example 16.5. The Flam Tap in Musical Context

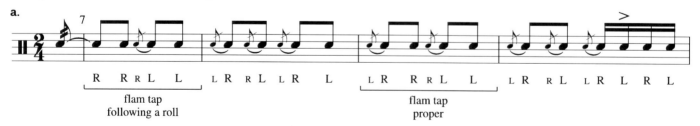

Here is another possibility, the **altered flam accent.**

Example 16.6. The Altered Flam Accent

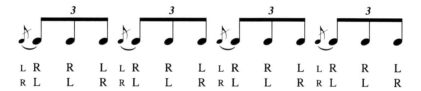

Play the flam-accent figures above. Start slowly, and "make" each stroke with an individual hand action.

Now, gradually increase the speed, and *open the flams* (with wider spacing) until the grace notes are given the same time value as the main notes. By giving them as much power as the main notes, you'll find you have merged from the flam accent figure into that of the long roll.

Example 16.7. The Altered Flam Accent Merged into the Long Roll

Increase the tempo to top speed, rebounding as speed permits, and then slow down as gradually as you sped up, merging the roll figure back into that of the flam accent.

The exercise may also be executed in the opposite manner by starting with the roll, merging into the flam-accent figure (as speed increases), and then coming back again. Or, it may be played at steady, even tempos, ranging from slow (enough to "make" each stroke), to fast (in which the rebound enters). There is nothing much to this exercise except to develop added control.

LESSON 17. **HOW HIGH THE HAT**

A St. Louis sideman once asked why the hi-hat beat, invariably written as shown in the figure below, is so seldom played exactly as written.

Example 17.1. Common Hi-Hat Rhythm

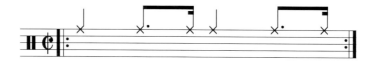

Many drum parts in modern dance music of the 1940s and '50s, particularly those considered standards, are more suggestive than literal. We are expected to play such parts as we feel, without necessarily following the notes. In fact, if a drummer were to play some of these parts exactly as written, their efforts would sound sad indeed. (Please remember that I'm referring to modern dance music of a specific era, not all music.)

More often than not we take the liberty of playing the hi-hat beat more "broadly," by using a triplet rhythm.

Example 17.2. The Broad Triplet on Hi-Hat

Here is a case in which the drummer doesn't follow the rhythm set down in the score; they follow that of the band. In other words, if a band adopts a broad rhythm, so should the drummer. Some bands adopt the broad, triplet rhythm unthinkingly; others cultivate it deliberately.

However, if everyone plays this rhythm in unison it is effective and, in my estimation, much more so than the stilted rhythm shown in the first figure.

In slow numbers, the drummer may back up a band with the double-dotted rhythm shown in Example 17.3. This is a wonderful **drive beat.**

Example 17.3. The Hi-Hat Drive Beat

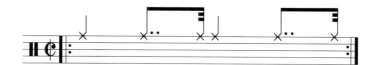

Still, another version of the hi-hat beat is the one most-often used when the tempo is faster than fast (just the plain rhythm, with no dots).

Example 17.4. A Fast Beat Hi-Hat Rhythm

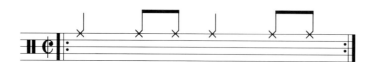

In a nutshell, the hi-hat is subject to any variation of distortion a player or band, through musical sense and experience, deems expedient. Of course, the precisely marked execution of the basic beat we learned earlier (the first figure) should be thoroughly mastered first. Then, from the firm foundation of metronomic exactitude, deviation to any desired degree will be found more easily.

You can create many sounds (colors) by opening and closing the hi-hat. Pressing your toe and lifting your heel will produce a tighter sound, while playing with the heel down will produce a lower pitch. You can open them slightly to "wash" the cymbals together, or you can play them wide open. You can also create numerous sounds by opening or closing the cymbals with the first finger and thumb of your left hand.

Opening and Closing Your Hi-Hat

Key:

○ = open hi-hat
+ = closed hi-hat
Ø = half-open hi-hat

Creating Colors on the Hi-Hat

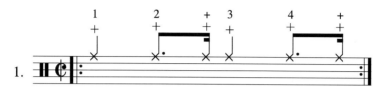

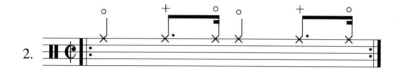

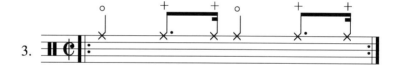

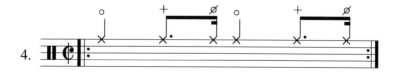

LESSON 18. SEXTUPLETS VERSUS TRIPLETS

What is the distinction between a sextuplet and a double triplet? The distinction is in their division/grouping. While the value of one sextuplet is the same as that of two triplets (using the same note values), it is customary to divide the sextuplet into groups of twos, whereas the double triplet clearly indicates six groups of twos. Since *Sensational Sid* was intended as a rudimental showpiece, I took the liberty of adding accents to the sextuplet to give it a rudimental syncopation. It is similar to syncopation in jazz music; in orchestra or band music I would divide sextuplets, in the absence of marked accents, into groups of twos.

However, there is plenty of opportunity here for confusion, both in accenting and beaming. More than a few writers employ sextuplets and triplets interchangeably, expecting a grouping of three in either case. Thus, the beaming of the sextuplet as commonly written is not always sufficiently clear to tell a player what a composer or writer may have had in mind. It might help if the writer uses something similar to the beaming on this example when the player could possibly interpret the sextuplet correctly. Nothing new or radical here, but such a marking leaves nothing to chance.

Example 18.1. Sextuplets and Triplets

beamed in threes   commonly written   beamed in twos

Among drummers who continue to play in the now ancient rudimental style, a common version of the sextuplet uses a heavy accent on the first note without any inner

divisions. Although alternate stickings can be used, it is most effective when executed with the double paradiddle, which, rudimentally, carries only one accent.

Example 18.2. Common Sextuplet

R L R L R R L R L R L L   R ʀ L ʟ R

Sextuplet and Triplet Exercises for Control

The following exercises are designed to develop control of the sextuplet by itself, as well as combined with the triplet. Preliminary practice should be done with heavy artificial accents as your guide. In later practice, these heavy accents should be replaced with light accents. In an actual playing situation, a musically sensitive and well-schooled drummer should take care not to stress the

subordinate divisions so as to make the sextuplet too conspicuous. In many instances, especially when playing faster tempos, the student will not stress them at all. But, the percussionist should think into a figure of this type and, in doing so, find they have "trained and well-controlled sticks" to mark its character, blend into the ensemble, and satisfy the conductor's desires.

Triplet and Sextuplet Exercises for Control

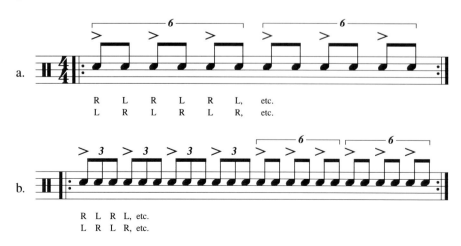

a.

R   L   R   L   R   L,   etc.
L   R   L   R   L   R,   etc.

b.

R L R L, etc.
L R L R, etc.

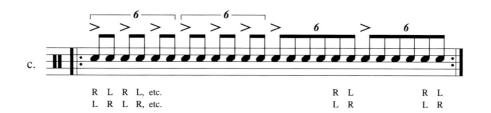

Sensational Sid

This next exercise, *Hot Shot!*, is an example of triplets and sextuplets utilizing both accents and dynamics.

Hot Shot!

NOTE: The numbers 7 or 9, above the rolls, indicate the numbered roll that is normally played in that instance— either a double-stroke or buzz roll. These suggested rolls may change depending on the tempo of the exercise.

LESSON 19. **THE SIDE TRIPLET**

(A Triplet Figure Repeated with the Same Sticking)

Here is an interesting rudiment not included in the "original 26." The **side triplet** is executed "to one side," and its most common sticking is either RRL RRL or RLL RLL (and reverse).

The following exercise may be played with either naturally accented or artificial accents.

Sticking

A	RRL RRL RRL RRL	RRL / / / (repeat 20 times)
(or)	LLR LLR LLR LLR	LLR / / /
B	RLL RLL RLL RLL	RLL / / /
(or)	LRR LRR LRR LRR	LRR / / /
(or)	RRR LLL RRR LLL	RRR / / /

Stress on the first note of each triplet can range from the tightest of natural accents (of varying degrees) to the heaviest of artificial accents. This type of sticking is to the drummer what triple tonguing is to the brass soloist, and it could be referred to as **triple sticking**. Its use in art music is rare, and it is generally restricted to passages in which it is specifically called for. Side triplets really shine when they are utilized in modern jazz solos and breaks.

In this context, they are brilliant and may be executed at high speed. The main difficulty in their use is that uneven sticking is apt to result in uneven rhythm. At best, triple sticking (like triple tonguing) possesses a characteristic lilt, which is why the symphonic conductor frowns upon the side triplet. However, when called for, this rudiment can be quite effective.

Other Ways to Get Started

RRL	R	RRL	R	RRL	RRL	R
LLR	L	LLR	L	LLR	LLR	L
RLL	R	RLL	R	RLL	RLL	R
LRR	L	LRR	L	LRR	LRR	L

Now, mix alternating and side triplets, and try to make one style sound as even as the other.

Alternating	**Side**
RLR LRL RLR LRL	RLL RLL RLL RLL (repeat 20 times)
LRL RLR LRL RLR	LRR LRR LRR LRR
RLR LRL RLR LRL	RRR LLL RRR LLL

Now that you've got the idea, go back and make up your own combinations.

LESSON 20. **INTERPRETING THE SINGLE AND DOUBLE DRAGS**

The combination of rhythm, grace notes, and accents in a series of single drags presents a problem to the drum author notating them in an exact, yet easy-to-read style. Consequently, the average author approximates such rudiments in their drum parts, and so we find ourselves given wide latitude in their interpretation.

Examples A and B below show how the average drum author approximates the single drags in binary measure. If true single drags are intended, such notation is misleading and, if played as written, will result in a disjointed rhythm, far from the one intended. Therefore, taking the latitude implied, we shrug our shoulders, play them as single drags drummer-style (as shown in examples C and D below), and hope for the best.

Example D approximates the slight hesitation before attacking the grace notes affected by many professional exhibitionists in traditional drumming. This is a highly personalized and brilliant style, requiring good control and timing.

Example E shows a jazz version of the rudiment fitted into an **alla breve** measure against the beat. The grace notes here are played as principal notes, struck from the normal striking level, and the rhythmic pattern follows the notation with exactitude.

Single Drag Exercises

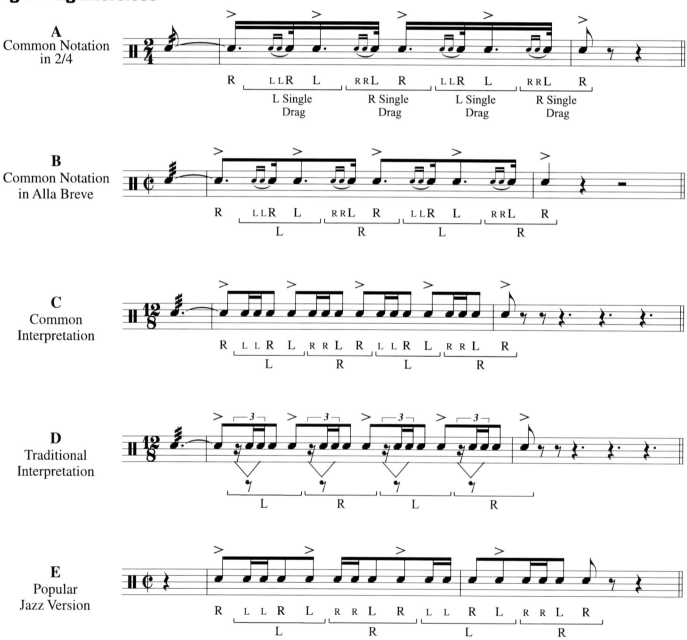

Interpreting the Double Drag

The **double drag** is another traditional rudiment. It is particularly effective when playing **6/8** rhythms in march tempo, brilliant when used in rudimental solos, and appears in such Camp Duty drumbeats as *The Dinner Call* and *Dusky Night.* It is not very adaptable to the binary beat of jazz and, in traditional form, rarely (if ever) appears in art music. However, for the rudimental drummer it's a must and, for the non-rudimental drummer, it should be mastered for the sense of accomplishment.

The combination of rhythm, grace notes, and accents in a series of double drags presents the same notation challenge to the drum author as the single drag does. This writer approximates double drags in his drum parts and, similarly, we find ourselves given wide latitude in their interpretation.

Example A below shows a common notation for the double drag applied to a **6/8** measure.

Example B shows the rhythm-frame of the rudiment without the embellishing grace notes.

Example C shows the frame more fully developed, while in Example D the common interpretation of the rudiment appears with the grace notes fully opened.

The traditional interpretation (Example E) includes the same slight hesitation before attacking the grace notes as that of the traditional single drag. This is the double drag of the "old timer"—one of the showiest and, at the same time, one of the most difficult rudiments in the book.

Example F illustrates a free-and-easy version with the grace notes being played as normal notes, struck from a normal striking level.

Double Drag Exercises

LESSON 21. ALLA BREVE

The question of the day is, should the **alla breve** signature be counted in two or in four?

$$\mathbf{C} = \text{in II or IV?}$$

This is a borderline signature that may be summed up and played as either a two- or four-beat measure, according to the way it is used.

If we don't dig too far back into the archives, the *alla breve* signature denotes quick, duple time, with the half note as the beat—**2/2** instead of **4/4**. In this phase, it calls for the same sound and rhythmic swing as its counterpart in **2/4**.

Alla Breve in Common and Cut-Time

Here, using either figure, the signature and tempo marking indicate the same two beats to the measure. In the case of a marching tune, for instance, these two beats will serve to mark the steps of marching soldiers at the U.S. troop cadence of 120 steps per minute. As you can see, the only difference in the figures above is the manner in which they are notated; and, this could simply be a matter of a composer's preference.

Now let's jump from the marching tune to popular dance music of the 1940s and '50s. This is different—so much

different! Most of it is scored in the four-beat rhythm of present-day jazz. Current composers and arrangers almost invariably score their brain-children in what the purists still stoutly maintain to be the two-beat signature of *alla breve*. An example of this appears below, showing the definite four-beat rhythm (marked in this instance by the bass drum), scored under the *alla breve* signature.

Swing Rhythm in Alla Breve

It makes very little difference to anyone playing which signature is used. The player knows that a four-beat rhythmic "feel" definitely calls for a four-beat count, regardless of the fine points of the signature.

Don't look now, but here's another thought for you. There *is* such a thing as contemporary music played with

a two-beat rhythm. Quite a lot of it, in fact. Here, you really count and think in two.

NOTE (Joe Morello): During my time studying with "Larry Stone," all the cut-time exercises in his *Stick Control* book were counted in **4/4.**

LESSON 22. **THE FINGER ROLL**

Do I approve of the **finger roll** or, as it is often called, *finger bounce*, wherein the wrists remain quiet and the sticks are moved by a single finger of each hand? I certainly do. Although this is a highly personal style, it is a very effective one. Of course, finger motion is nothing new, as most of us incorporate coordinated finger movements in our respective handholds and have been doing so for as long

as I can remember. Then, too, some of us use callisthenic movements to develop and limber up the muscles of the fingers and hands. But, presenting finger motion by itself as an accomplishment is a new phase, developed within the last few years, in the drumming world, and one that has added a bit of showmanship to the modern drummer's bag of tricks.

Finger Control Workouts

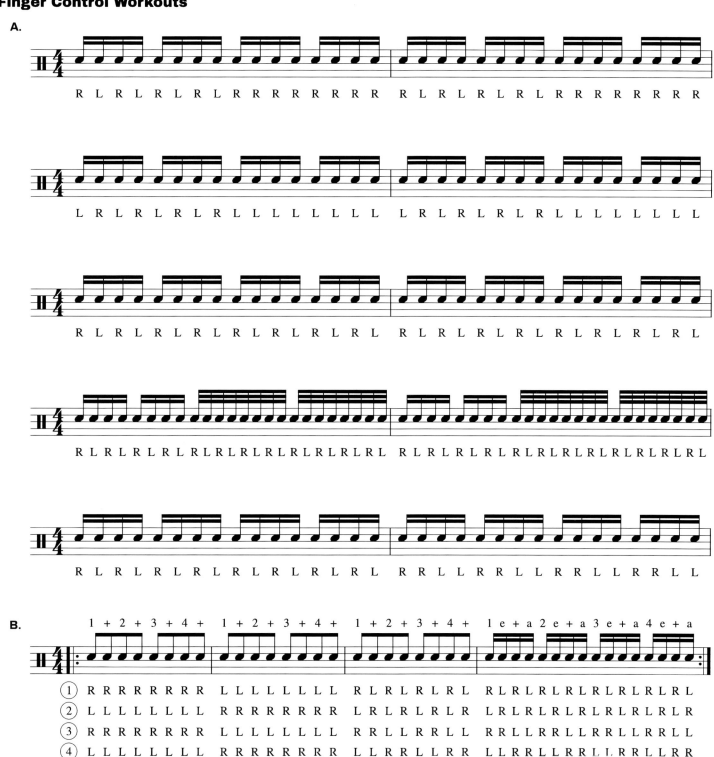

More Finger-Control Exercises

This exercise will help your concentration when you're playing a descending/ascending number of finger bounces (from 12 to 1, and then back to 12 with each hand). Keep a steady pulse without rests, and play from line to line without stopping.

NOTE: When counting to 12 in the following example (and others), please count:

"1 2 3 4 5 6 SEV 8 9 10 LEV 12" so that all numbers have only one syllable.

The Hourglass

```
LLLLLLLLLLLLRRRRRRRRRRRR
LLLLLLLLLLLRRRRRRRRRRR
LLLLLLLLLLRRRRRRRRRR
LLLLLLLLLRRRRRRRRR
LLLLLLLLRRRRRRRR
LLLLLLLRRRRRRR
LLLLLLRRRRRR
LLLLLRRRRR
LLLLRRRR
LLLRRR
LLRR
LR
LLRR
LLLRRR
LLLLRRRR
LLLLLRRRRR
LLLLLLRRRRRR
LLLLLLLRRRRRRR
LLLLLLLLRRRRRRRR
LLLLLLLLLRRRRRRRRR
LLLLLLLLLLRRRRRRRRRR
LLLLLLLLLLLRRRRRRRRRRR
LLLLLLLLLLLLRRRRRRRRRRRR
```

LESSON 23. **LEFT-HAND VELOCITY**

Just a few comments regarding the fabulous left-hand speed attained by pupil Joe Morello.

In a nutshell, his speed was attained through long and diligent practice. This practice was augmented from a strictly rudimental foundation, incorporating plenty of hand-to-hand work through *Stick Control,* plus many handwritten special assignments designed to further develop wrist and finger bounce control of the weaker hand.

A sample of the latter exercises that were written expressly for Joe follows. You may find the exercises helpful in building up your own wrist and fingers.

Since the following exercise is designed primarily for control of one stick, you will need to depart from the customarily well-balanced poising levels for which we strive, and strike the one stick from a higher level than the other (at a medium speed, from a 9-inch level for the left stick against a 5-inch level for the right).

Play through the entire routine, and repeat each figure many times before moving on to the next line. Take 30 minutes to finish the routine without stopping. I suggest you start at a medium playing tempo. As your control improves, increase the tempo up to a maximum without distorting the beats.

If you are a "lefty," the routine may be transposed to "right-hand velocity" and practiced to develop your weaker hand.

In addition to speed and control, many other factors contribute to the making of a fine, proficient drummer. These, as well as speed and control, are best learned through personal instruction by a qualified teacher. I suggest you contact the best teacher in your area and place yourself in their hands. Through personal knowledge, a competent teacher will quickly be able to answer the many questions that cannot be thoroughly answered through correspondence or the pages of a magazine.

Joe Fingers

LESSON 24. **BREAKS AND SOLOS**

The last time New York ace drum instructor Ted Reed visited the Stone Studio, he played some snappy four-measure drum breaks on the studio drumset—some of which he used in his teaching. I suggested that he write out a couple of them and send them to me for reprinting. He did, and here they are. Many thanks, Ted.

Here is a four-measure break by Ted Reed.

Example 24.1. Four-Measure Break

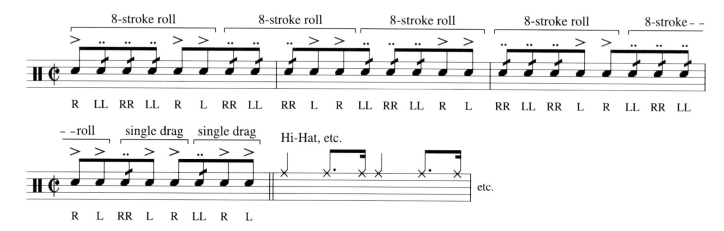

Four-Measure Break Exercises

Here are a few four-measure breaks to add to your collection.

Here are a few two-measure breaks to add to your collection.

Two-Measure Break Exercises

Create Your Own Break

Now the question becomes, "How can I create my own breaks?" Simple. Start by selecting a favorite rhythm pattern. Here is a two-measure pattern to begin with.

Then, add accents.

Add some grace notes.

Finally, fill in the empty spots with bass drum beats, change the accents to rim shots, and speed up the tempo. Now you have a playable two-measure break.

Add two to make four.

To make a four-measure break using the above, create a simple two-measure figure ahead of it.

Modern Drumset Soloing

In a magazine article, Joe Morello referred to the extension of his on-the-set solos as a continuous line (as if they were compositions). Let's examine exactly what this means and how it's done.

> **This refers to the streamlining of short phrases (rhythmic patterns, to the drummer) into longer ones, or, possibly, into an uninterrupted sequence—a smooth, flowing continuity of inspirational rhythmic conception.**

Such phrasing represents the finished product. It is the culmination of a stepwise progression of study in which short phrases come first. Let's say the beginning soloist starts out with a series of two-measure breaks. These are simply written and considered corny. The student learns to execute them first on a pad and then on the drumset. To fully comprehend the rhythmic structure, the student is taught to count aloud as they execute the two-measure breaks (this oral count proves to be a life-saver when, later, in longer and more involved breaks, they may be called on to confine a solo to a specified number of measures). Now, by combining two, two-measure breaks, they enter the four-measure stage. Then they combine two fours into an eight, and so on.

By this time the student is stringing their *twos, fours,* etc. together like a string of sausages, without much thought of an unbroken line. This procedure might be compared with the way a baby builds a toy house with blocks—one block at a time.

Somewhere along the way the student is encouraged to improve upon and add to the structure of the breaks they've created up to this point. They are now encouraged to improvise on these basic patterns with thoughts of their own—to disregard basic patterns entirely if so inspired.

And, from here they may gradually develop and perfect a creative ability that inspires them to solo in their own right and from their own thoughts. In other words, *from inspiration.*

Once the beginning drummer has accumulated their arsenal of two-, four- and eight-bar solos, they can *string them together* to create the drum solo called for in a particular song. Still, the masterpiece needs to be placed appropriately, and the drummer needs to be able to recognize the *form* of the song they are playing.

Let's discuss some common **song forms.** First, and the simplest, is the 12-bar blues (repeated to equal 24 measures). Easily recognized for its three-chord structure, drum solos can be structured using three, four-bar phrases per 12-bar chorus, or any multiple of two-bar solos to fit the needs of the particular song.

Next is the **verse-chorus form.** This consists of two sections, usually equaling 32 measures. Here again these sections are all divisible by two or four. The verse and chorus have different melodies and chords, and are often broken down into a 16-bar verse and a 16-bar chorus.

Finally, you will be dealing with the so-called AABA form, again totaling 32 measures broken down into four, eight-measure sections. All the A sections repeat the same melody and harmony for each eight-measure section, but the one B section (called the "Bridge" or "Release") contains a different melody and harmony. Certainly there are, and will be in the future, other song forms that we will be called upon to recognize and master. This is just a start. As a *musical drummer* you will need to perfect your solos so you are able to enrich the very essence of the song you are playing.

LESSON 25. EMBELLISHMENTS WITH GRACE NOTES

Below is a series of notes and embellishments for the snare drum, arranged in exercise form for the development of two-handed technique. The indicated sticking is not intended to conflict with any system an individual may have adopted for actual playing. Rather, it is designed to emphasize the point that the hands should be fully trained to execute grace notes as they appear; in snare drum technique, such grace notes are to be employed without disturbing either the rhythm, power, or an established sticking of the principal notes that they precede.

Embellishments with Grace Notes

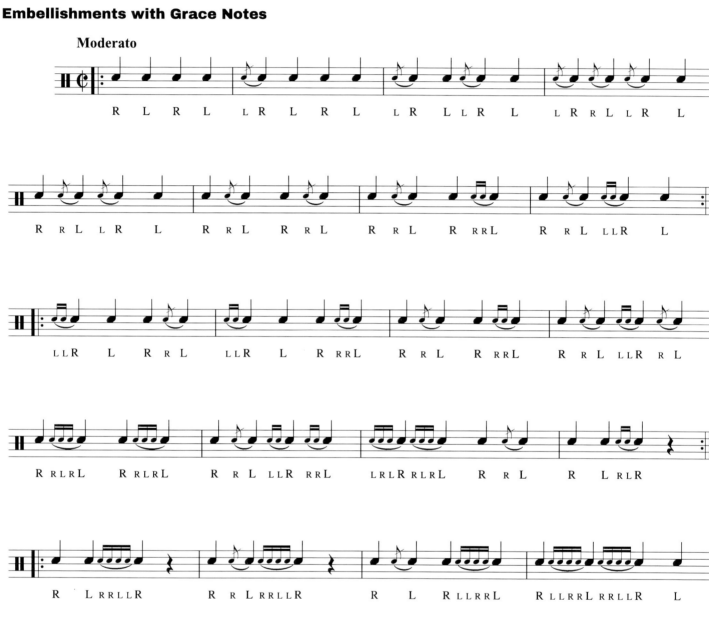

R L Ll rr L L R   R   L l l r r L L R   R rr L L rr L R L   R rr L L rr L   R LL rr L

R   L   R   L   R   L   R L   R L   R   L   R   L   R

Embellishments with Grace Notes in 6/8

L L R L R rr L   L R L R L R L L R L R L   rr L R L R L R L R L R L

R L R rr L R L   L L R   L R L R   L L R L rr L rr L   R   L L R L R L rr L rr L   R

L L R   L L R L rr L   rr L   R   L L R L R L rr L   R   R   L L R L rr L   rr L   R

R L R L rr L rr L   R   R L R L   R L R L   R L R L   R L R L R L R L R L

LESSON 26. **DOTTED NOTES**

In a letter to me, a Midwestern instructor weeps, wails, and beats their chest in despair over the inability to convince some of their mallet-playing pupils that dotted notes should be played as written. They complain that the average conception of this notation among their students (a different appellation was used in the letter, but never mind) seems to be limited to *dum da dum da dum*, with the accent on the *dum*. They wonder what to do and if other instructors have similar trouble.

They certainly do, as the average student isn't interested enough in the precise placement of notes using dotted rhythms to give this important element the careful study and practice it entails. Yet there is something to be said for the student at that; in much of the lighter music of today, dotted notes don't have to be—and are not expressed— in their exact notated form. But, in longhair music, the longhair dot is definitely called for, and to the serious student, mastering it isn't particularly difficult.

The first and simplest approach to exactitude in dotting, especially for the percussionist, is mathematical breakdown, reinforced by oral count.

For instance, the dotted notes in Example 26.1 are broken down using sixteenth notes.

Example 26.1. Dotted Notes

And here is an even more "longhair" example of a double-dotted eighth note with a thirty-second note.

Example 26.2. Dotted Thirty-Second Notes

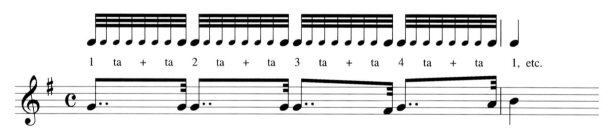

And, if the student studies this binary breakdown painstakingly, *counting aloud* as they do so, they soon will be able to execute "dots" with exactitude. (That's if they don't consider such an elementary approach too trivial to deserve their attention.)

Learning by Contrast

Another approach to dots involves the student playing a figure like Example 26.1, but in contrasting ternary breakdowns.

Example 26.3. Ternary Breakdown

This, by the way, is the rhythm they are apt to fall into, carelessly, in the fond belief that they actually are playing in the binary rhythm of Example 26.1. By implementing the contrast, they will further learn to differentiate between the two figures.

And, Still More

I would suggest that recalcitrant students work on the final example below, and add similar ones that may come to mind. Throw in some double dots for good measure, pick out your favorite sticking, and see if you don't get gratifying results.

Example 26.4. Contrasting Dotted-Note Rhythms

For drumsticks or mallets

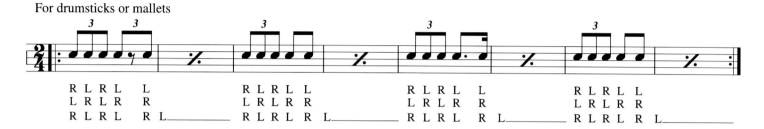

R L R L	L	R L R L L	R L R L	L	R L R L L
L R L R	R	L R L R R	L R L R	R	L R L R R
R L R L	R L_____	R L R L R L_____	R L R L	R L_____	R L R L R L_____

LESSON 27. MUSICAL TEMPERAMENT

I believe that the true artist has temperament, and that music and emotion are closely related. I also believe that the inspired, imaginative drummer plays from the soul. When they do, there is fire, life, and spirit in their execution. They feel—and, in doing so, radiate—dynamics. On the other hand, the drummer who plays "callisthenically" does not ring the bell.

Diversifying Practice

Today we are asked to perform in ways that we never dreamed of. Therefore, it is necessary to diversify practice. For example, in order to develop a light touch, we must practice with lightness in mind. Similarly, for delicate handling we must strive for the delicate touch in practice. One of the most difficult rolls to master, long or short, is the pure two-beat roll played *pianissimo* with the tip of the sticks striking from not more than an inch or so above the drumhead. This calls for specialized practice and plenty of it. Not too many players have had the patience to perfect this roll.

From George Stone: The following two paragraphs, taken from the foreword of my practice textbook, *Stick Control*, expands on the thought of diversifying your practice:

"A word to the orchestral drummer: Do not let the word 'rudimental' frighten you nor prevent you from putting in a normal amount of practice on power, high-hand practice, and the open roll. This will not spoil the light touch, delicate shading, or fine-grained effects demanded of you in modern musical interpretation. To the contrary, by achieving better control of the sticks, it will enable you to produce even finer and more delicate effects than heretofore.

"Likewise, a word to the rudimental drummer: Do not hesitate to devote a portion of your practice period to lightness and touch, and especially to the playing of the closed roll. For if your practice is confined entirely to power and endurance, your execution will become one-sided, heavy, and clumsy. Suffice it to say, practice in lighter execution will, by giving you a fuller control of the sticks, help your power, endurance, and speed."

Barry James: Now, since this blurb should appear at the end of a year, when new resolutions are recklessly being made among the practicing fraternity of drummers, the following suggestions might serve to set some of the cool weather enthusiasts on the right track.

Practice regularly: Set aside a certain time each day, and adhere strictly to your schedule. One hour each day is better than three hours one day and nothing the next. Regularity is indispensable in the training of mind and muscle.

Practice sufficiently: This varies with each individual, but, in my estimation, one hour is the minimum. If you can't spare this time, don't expect to set the world afire, regardless of whether you're a beginner or expert.

Concentrate: The value of the practice period is not computed by the time consumed, but by the time *employed.*

Practice on the pad, as well as on the drumset: It is on the practice pad that you learn to execute the figures that you later apply on the set.

Practice what you don't know: Continuing to practice material you have mastered last week or last month doesn't help your progress. Sure you can review a drumset groove, your rudiments, or a particular musical etude, but spend most of your valuable practice time working on challenging new material.

Check your grip frequently: Don't make the mistake of employing one grip for practice and another for actual playing. If you're determined to adopt some outlandish position on the set, use the same position on the pad.

Practice versus playing: In practice, follow the rules of the textbook meticulously. In playing, take the license of playing *as you feel, as the composer intended, or as your leader directs*, according to the character of the music. In other words, the textbook shows the ideal way, while your judgment, gained through experience, tells you the way of expediency.

Stone emphasized dividing your practice time into segments. Let's say you have one hour put aside each day for "musical improvement." You could break down your hour as follows: warm-up and stretching (5 minutes), rudimental workout (5 minutes), stick and foot technique, i.e., *Stick Control, Accents and Rebounds, Master Studies*, etc. (10 minutes), snare drum, mallets, or drumset reading

(10 minutes), new drumset grooves (10 minutes), playing along to recordings or working on difficult material (20 minutes), etc. At first this may not seem like enough time to get everything accomplished in a given day, but cumulatively you will see progress over time.

This, of course, is only one suggestion. Each drummer will set up their own practice schedule depending on their individual goals. And finally, as George Lawrence Stone said:

"Set your musical goals, and practice to accomplish them."

LESSON 28. **PHONETICS**

Toy Boat

This little tongue-twister starred as the pièce de résistance during the parlor game era. But now it can serve as a good conditioner for the sluggish tongue if you have trouble counting aloud during practice.

All you have to do is say, "Toy boat, toy boat, toy boat," as long, loud, and fast as you can. When your tongue can get around this little gimmick without falling into something that sounds like *toe boit, toe boit, toe boit*, you should be able to count in your practice routine as never before.

Wind instrument players usually don't have much trouble with a thing like this; the player's tongue is already sharpened by daily practice of the instrument. But the drummer—well, try it yourself and see what happens.

Here are some of the vocalizations Stone taught his students in order to help them *feel* the sound of the rudiments.

Long Roll (Double Stroke)	*Say:* Ma-Ma Da-Da *or* Dou-ble Dou-ble
Single Paradiddle	*Say:* Par-a-did-dle
Double Paradiddle	*Say:* Par-a Par-a Did-dle
Triple Paradiddle	*Say:* Par-a Par-a Par-a Did-dle
Single Paradiddle-diddle	*Say:* Par-a Did-dle Did-dle
Flam	*Say:* Fl-am
Flam Tap	*Say:* Flam-Tap
Flam Accent	*Say:* Flam Ac-cent or Flam Trip-let
Flam Paradiddle	*Say:* Flam-a Did-dle
Flam Paradiddle-diddle	*Say:* Flam-a Did-dle Did-dle
Flamacue	*Say:* Flam BAM A Cue
Drag	*Say:* Go to Bed
Single Drag Tap	*Say:* Go to Bed Tom
Double Drag Tap	*Say:* Go to Bed, Go to Bed Tom
Lesson Twenty-Five	*Say:* Les-son Twen-ty Five
Drag Paradiddle # 1	*Say:* BAM Go to Bed A Did-dle
Drag Paradiddle #2	*Say:* BAM Go to Bed Go to Bed A Did-dle
Single Ratamacue	*Say:* It's A Rat-a-ma-CUE
Double Ratamacue	*Say:* It's A Rat, It's A Rat-a-ma-cue
Triple Ratamacue	*Say:* It's A Rat, It's A Rat, It's A Rat-a-ma-cue

LESSON 29. **TIMING SHORT ROLLS**

The following example shows the damage that short rolls played in **2/4** can do to the rhythmic flow of a band playing in **6/8**.

Example 29.1. Damaging Short-Roll

The 6/8 Band—The 2/4 Drummer!

There are those who would prefer using seven-stroke rolls in the above **2/4** and **6/8** examples. Then again, at a tempo slower than *bright*, seven-stroke rolls might be used more advantageously to fill the duration involved. There is no reason seven-stroke rolls shouldn't be used when they "fit." However, when any short roll must be started ahead of its notated value in order to get in all its beats, it definitely is not the roll for that purpose, and a roll of fewer beats should be substituted. The exception is, of course, certain roll standards in ancient drumming, wherein a great deal of latitude is often taken.

From George Stone: Remember that my book *Stick Control* contains many special exercises designed to help any anxious soul who yearns for self-improvement —to fix durative values more firmly in his/her mind, and to negotiate stroke rolls with greater ease and certainty.

The student and professional must dwell on careful versus careless timing of short rolls, viewed with virtuous indignation by the antics of the **2/4** *drummer in the* **6/8** *band*, and we end up by referring to a set of conditioning exercises of mine designed to facilitate short-roll execution.

The exercises below are taken from the set of conditioning exercises that Stone refers to above. They are based on timing the pattern of a given roll to the rhythm in which it is to be played with single-hand movements first and adding rebounds—the fill-in—after.

Their study and practice should aid the advanced percussion student by giving their short rolls the exact durative value called for in the score.

The rolls in these exercises are the rudimental short rolls of five and seven beats respectively (*stroke rolls*, also called by C. E. Gardner, *rolls of trim*), which start before a beat and end with an accent on that beat or another one. These are among the rolls often used at and around the marching tempo, which, prior to the glorification of the fast-stepping school band, centered around 120 beats per minute. Of course, the student should practice the exercises at slow tempos first, gradually stepping up the speed thereafter to a much faster tempo.

The rolls are playable both in the open, two-beat style, and in the buzz, but with the emphasis on the former. The term *commonly written* denotes just one way in which the rolls might be notated. Some of the stickings are logical—some are not—but all help to develop perception and control.

The first exercise shows five-stroke rolls following the long-roll pattern. The five-stroke pattern itself is established in the first two measures of this exercise (and of the following exercises) by the single-hand movements of the rolls. The fill-in to complete the rolls appears in the next two measures. A common way of notating the figure follows. Stroke rolls here end "on the beat," with such natural accents as indicated by the time signature. In practice, it is a good idea to occasionally use heavier accents.

Exercise 29.2. Five-Stroke Rolls with Accents in 6/8

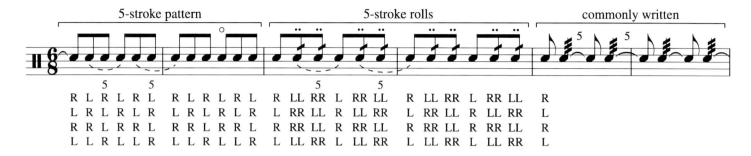

Next come the same five strokes, but now in **2/4**. When executed at the same playing tempo, the rolls here must be of shorter duration than those above.

Exercise 29.3. Five-Stroke Rolls with Accents in 2/4

The same rolls in **6/8** must be of even shorter duration.

Exercise 29.4. Five-Stroke Rolls in 6/8

Exercise 29.5, if and when executed with five-stroke rolls (a debatable selection for bright tempos), really reduces their duration to a minimum.

Exercise 29.5. Up-Tempo Five-Stroke Rolls

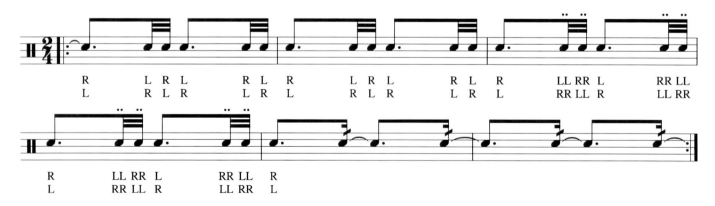

The following exercises feature seven-stroke rolls instead of five-stroke rolls. Often, and especially at tempos slower than bright, seven-stroke rolls will fill a given duration better than five-stroke rolls. Most important, however, is the fact that stroke rolls, irrespective of the number of beats, should be started at the beginning of their duration, and neither before nor after. The purpose of the following exercises is to develop skill in doing just that.

Exercise 29.6. Up-Tempo Seven-Stroke Rolls

Exercise 29.7. More Up-Tempo Seven-Stroke Rolls

Exercise 29.8 Still More Up-Tempo Seven-Stroke Rolls

LESSON 30. **COUNTING THE NUMBERED ROLLS AND THE NEW NUMBERED (COMPOUND) ROLLS**

George Lawrence Stone taught me a simple method to count all the numbered rolls. I've added the rolls not included in the original 26 Standard Rudiments, but that are in general use today. Stone was one of the founders of the National Association of Rudimental Drummers and served as its president for many years. Stone's counting goes beyond the double-stroke numbered rolls (NARD), but also includes a counting method for both the single-stroke and buzz rolls (now known as **multiple-stroke or buzz rolls**).

As Stone's students, we would often receive handouts, which were handwritten exercises of material he was working on. He would ask us to study the material and give him our feedback. One of the handouts I received contained the "new" or "compound rolls," including single, double, and buzz rolls. These even-numbered rolls are

the eight-, twelve-, fourteen-, and sixteen-stroke rolls. The now accepted six- and ten-stroke rolls are listed under the standard rolls. All rolls, including the standard and new compound rolls, are included in the following pages.

NOTE: Be aware that some rudimental rolls alternate from hand to hand. Others start and continue with the same hand (either right or left) each time they are played in sequence.

For our purposes, the single, double, and buzz rolls included in this lesson are marked with a "then" if they are to be alternated, or with an "or" if they are to start with the same hand each time you continue the roll. "Or" simply means that you can start (and continue) the roll with either hand, but don't alternate it.

Exercise 30.1 Counting Single-Stroke Rolls

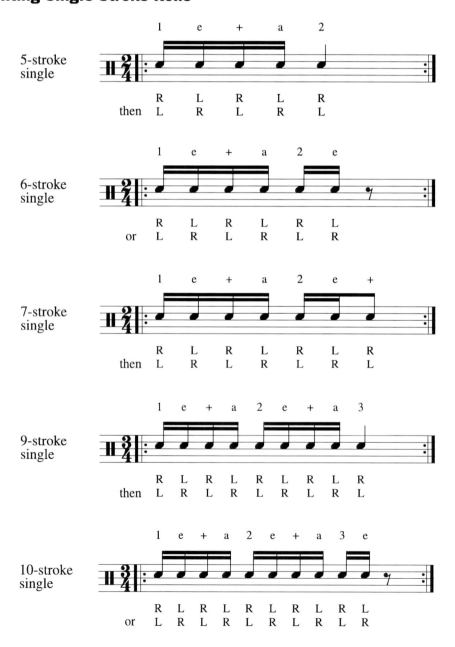

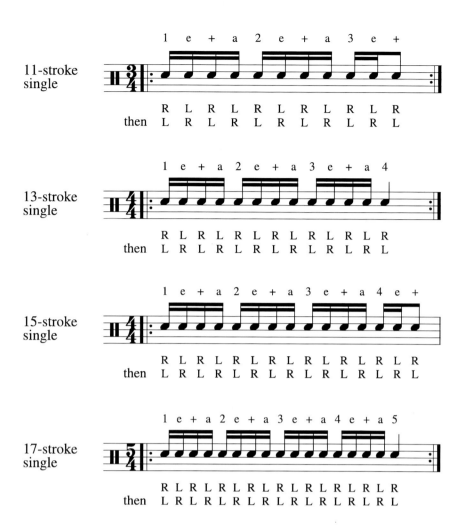

Exercise 30.2 Counting the New Single-Stroke Rolls

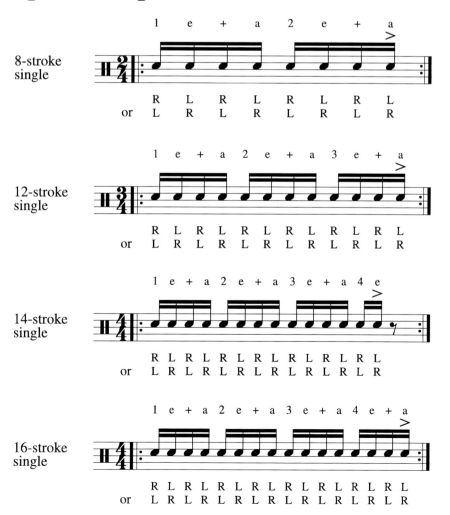

Exercise 30.3 Counting Double-Stroke Rolls

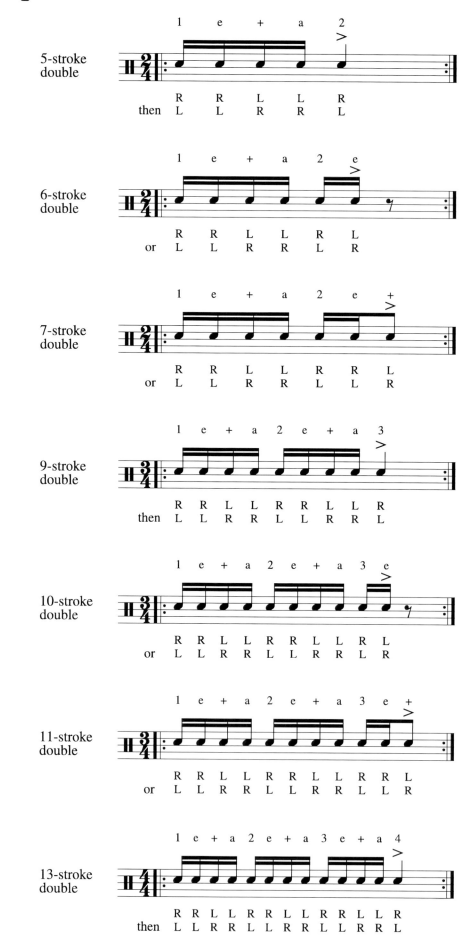

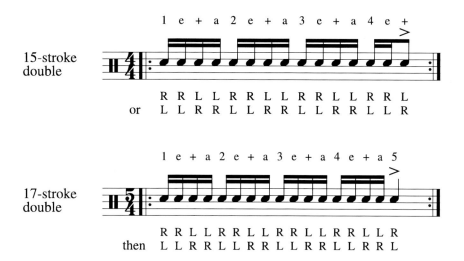

15-stroke double

1 e + a 2 e + a 3 e + a 4 e +

R R L L R R L L R R L L R R L
or L L R R L L R R L L R R L L R

17-stroke double

1 e + a 2 e + a 3 e + a 4 e + a 5

R R L L R R L L R R L L R R L L R
then L L R R L L R R L L R R L L R R L

Exercise 30.4 Counting the New Double-Stroke Rolls

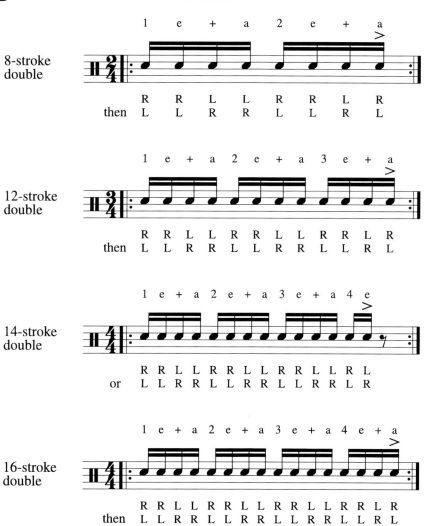

8-stroke double

1 e + a 2 e + a

R R L L R R L R
then L L R R L L R L

12-stroke double

1 e + a 2 e + a 3 e + a

R R L L R R L L R R L R
then L L R R L L R R L L R L

14-stroke double

1 e + a 2 e + a 3 e + a 4 e

R R L L R R L L R R L L R L
or L L R R L L R R L L R R L R

16-stroke double

1 e + a 2 e + a 3 e + a 4 e + a

R R L L R R L L R R L L R R L R
then L L R R L L R R L L R R L L R L

Exercise 30.5 Counting Multiple-Bounce (Buzz) Rolls

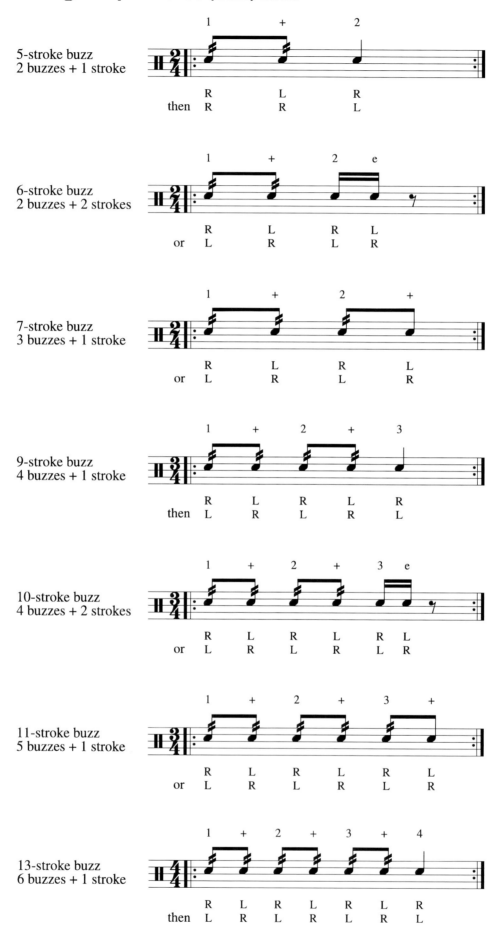

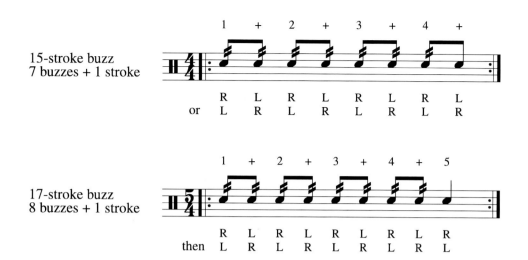

Exercise 30.6 Counting the New Multiple-Bounce (Buzz) Rolls

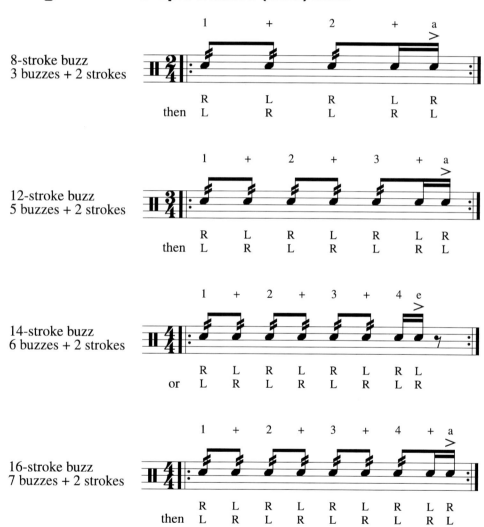

LESSON 31. **WORDS OF WISDOM/ANSWERING A FEW QUESTIONS**

Drumming in Two Easy Lessons

A reader writes: "A brother drummer claims there are only two rudiments in drumming, the single stroke and the double stroke, and that these are all you have to know, not all 26 rudiments. Is this right?"

Yes, reader, it's right as far as it goes. Tell the brother there are only 26 letters in the alphabet, and that all he has to know is A and B until he finds out all 26 letters have to be strung together in some sort of way before they make sense. How many words can he string together just using A and B?

Slow Practice First

Answering a letter: "I judge from your letter that you are practicing your single-stroke roll and allied figures at overly fast tempos. Consequently, your playing muscles get tied into knots, and your beats become distorted."

Again, I can't emphasize this enough. Go back to slower tempos in your practice for a while. Strange as it may seem, ultimate speed with the drumsticks is developed only from a background of practice at the slower tempos.

In a nutshell, you must first practice at slow-motion tempos for *precision*; next, at normal tempos for *endurance*; then, and only then, with precision controlled and endurance developed, are you prepared to practice for *speed itself*. This is it in a nutshell, but the orderly progression outlined above is a must.

The Wheat from the Chaff

An eager seeker, after more light on the whys and wherefores of percussion, beats his chest in despair over the conflict of opinion apparent in the writings of various drum authorities.

Don't let it disturb you, friend. Conflict, or difference of opinion, is and always will be with us, and it is only through the aforementioned that a meeting of the minds on any given subject will finally, we hope, be achieved. Get information on your favorite subject from all sources, then separate the wheat from the chaff, and settle for whatever meeting of the minds you may detect.

Love Your Practice Pad

"Love your drums!" says a well-known professional. "Otherwise they'll not do their best for you." "Ain't it the truth!" comments G.L.S. "But before you can get your drums to fully respond, you've got to do a whale of a lot of loving on that old practice pad."

A very young drummer with big-time aspirations is apt to disregard the importance of the pad. They become so fascinated with the sounds they get from their drumset while practicing with records that they fail to allot a due amount of time to their daily study and practice of the basics—but, sounds can be no better than *production*, which means control of rhythm, *without the distractions of musical accompaniment.*

Practice the Things You Don't Like

Ten to one the reason you don't like it is because you can't do it. Drummers often waste precious time over some easy figure (or a difficult one they've already mastered) when they should really be working on rhythms that seem unattainable. Don't let your daily practice degenerate into an aimless banging around of sticks and mallets. Go after something tough, and don't let go until you own it.

The Perfect Roll

It is impossible to execute a two-beat (or its counterpart, the buzz) in unvaried power. This is despite what the unaided ear tells the listener: that they are hearing a "perfect" roll. There is no such thing as a perfect roll. The reason for imperfection is simple. The initial roll-stroke of either stick is *struck* by hand action. The following stroke (or strokes) is produced by *rebound*. As with bouncing a rubber ball to the floor, the initial impact produces a stroke of given power, *but* the rebounds that follow strike with correspondingly less power, one by one, until the ball finally comes to rest.

The same principle follows in the rebounding of drumsticks. If, with either sticks or a ball, we could make rebounds as strong in power as an initial impact, the sticks would rebound to perfection, the ball would bounce forever, and—*Look, Ma! We've discovered the secret of perpetual motion!*

A roll, either two-beat or buzz, may sound smooth because the beats follow one another too rapidly for the ear to detect irregularity, but irregularity is there, as is so clearly depicted by carbon-paper reproduction. Refer to the carbon paper test on page 17.

There is a similar irregularity in art if you want to look for it. Look at and admire a painting by some old master. Look at it from a distance of only a few feet, and you'll see more irregularities than picture. You will see what to the untrained eyes resembles nothing more than a messy mixture of many-hued brush marks apparently going no place. But then step back and enjoy the majesty.

LESSON 32. **STICK TWISTERS**

The following exercises are a nice study in contrasting rhythms, featuring quintuplets displacing normal groups of fours.

Quintuplet Exercises with Groups of Four

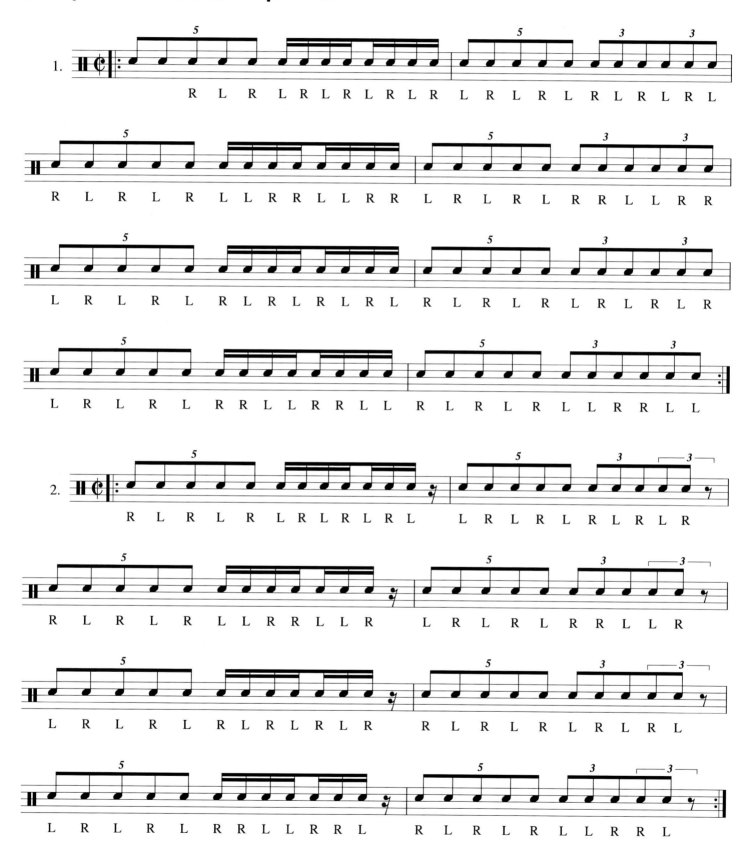

In the next two exercises, the normal four groups are displaced by sextuplets.

Quintuplet Exercises with Sextuplets

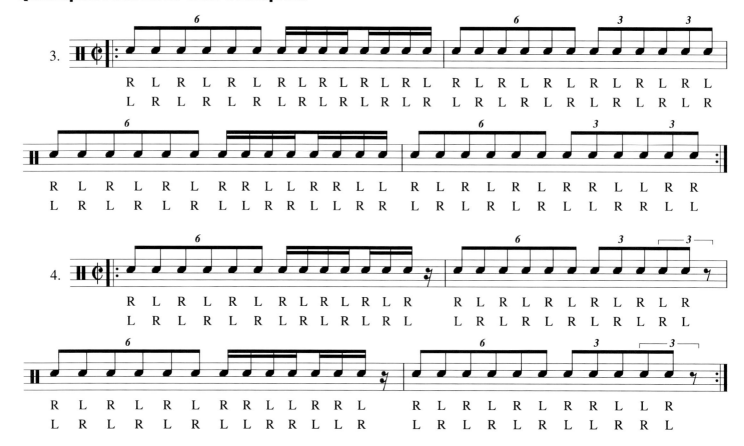

Although the sextuplet normally carries but one accent—a natural accent on its first note—its grouping is three times two, whereas the grouping of two triplets is two times three. Therefore, in order to fix the divisive contrast firmly in mind, you could practice Example 32.1 as a preparatory exercise to *Quintuplet Exercises with Sextuplets*. Accent heavily as marked, but remember: accenting the sextuplet would not occur in actual playing unless specifically called for.

Example 32.1. Stick Twisters with Accents

Finally, our stick twisters end up in a blaze of glory with septuplets now being the featured attraction.

HINT: Try counting the septuplets as such: 1234123.

More Stick Twisters

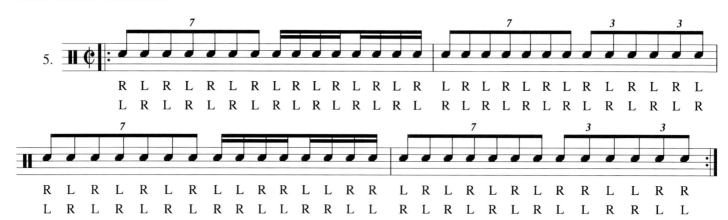

6.

| R | L | R | L | R | L | R | L | R | L | R | L | R | L | | L | R | L | R | L | R | L | R | L | R | L | R |
| L | R | L | R | L | R | L | R | L | R | L | R | L | R | | R | L | R | L | R | L | R | L | R | L | R | L |

| R | L | R | L | R | L | R | L | L | R | R | L | L | R | | L | R | L | R | L | R | L | R | R | L | L | R |
| L | R | L | R | L | R | L | R | R | L | L | R | R | L | | R | L | R | L | R | L | R | L | L | R | R | L |

CONCLUSION: **WHY ALL THIS GROUNDWORK?**

The question arises, "Is all this groundwork necessary?" Many a young drummer will say, "I never had to go through this step-by-step preparation. I picked up drumming as I went along. It came naturally to me, and I'm pretty good at it."

The answer is simple. "Pretty good" isn't enough in this era of keen competition and understanding audiences. A drum beat or solo today must be more than a spasmodic conglomeration of bumps and thumps banged down helter-skelter on a set of skins and cymbals. It must carry a message—a message inspired by the player's thoughts and clarified by their knowledge and application of rhythmic structure. And, this is where the preliminary training comes in.

"Careful, considered, and continued practice of such combinations offered here and in my books *Stick Control* and *Accents and Rebounds* will, with precise interpretation, aid in the development of 'a pair of smart hands.'"—*George Lawrence Stone*

We are what we repeatedly do. Excellence, therefore, is not an act but a habit. There is a growing realization in science that few people are born gifted. It takes time and persistence to be world class at anything. Always remember: You can be brilliant—you just must stick with whatever it is you want to be brilliant at.

"Do what you love, and love what you do."

Wishing you a lifetime of happy drumming.

Sincerely,
Barry James for
George Lawrence Stone
and Joe Morello

APPENDIX

Though this book includes new engravings of George Lawrence Stone's exercises, we thought it would be neat for you to see some of Stone's handwritten notation.

Longhair Dotted Note Exercise

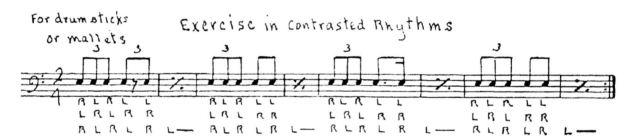

Contrasted Dots

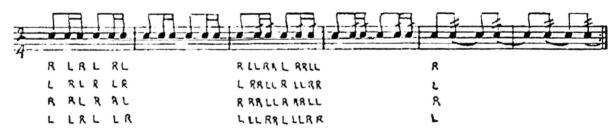

Dotted Note Contrasted Rhythms Exercise

Five-Stroke Rolls With Accents in 2/4

Five-Stroke Rolls With Accents in 6/8

Moderato

Embellishments With Grace Notes

The Flexible Roll

PHOTO GALLERY

George Lawrence Stone

Joe Morello and Barry James

1910 George Burt Stone
Concert Snare Drum

Vic Firth